Bird Island in Antarctic Waters

I dedicate this book to the Fids,
especially Peter, John, Bruce, and Nigel,
with the hope that it will help preserve
the close bond that has long existed
between the British Antarctic Survey
and the United States
Antarctic Research Program.

BIRD ISLAND IN ANTARCTIC WATERS

David F. Parmelee

UNIVERSITY OF MINNESOTA PRESS

MINNEAPOLIS

Published by the University of Minnesota Press,
2037 University Avenue Southeast,
Minneapolis, Minnesota 55414

Library of Congress Cataloging in Publication Data

Parmelee, David Freeland, 1924-
    Bird Island in Antarctic waters.

    Bibliography: p.
    Includes index.
    1. Birds — Antarctic regions — Bird Island. 2. Bird
Island, Antarctic regions. I. Title.
QL695.2.P37   598.2998'9   79-27456
ISBN 0-8166-0937-3
ISBN 0-8166-0940-3 pbk.

The University of Minnesota
is an equal-opportunity
educator and employer.

PREFACE AND ACKNOWLEDGMENTS

This book is not intended to be a scientific report, but rather a birding experience as seen through the eyes of a field biologist and illustrated for those who observe wildlife for recreational and aesthetic reasons. I leave the strictly scientific papers to my British colleagues who labor long and hard on Bird Island. My objectives and desires are to call attention to the ornithologic work being conducted on what my British friends call the most remarkable island for sea birds on this earth.

A note on the maps used in this book. To simplify them, I have listed only those place-names mentioned in the text. I had not been with my British companions long before realizing that they had several different Bird Island maps whose place-names varied from one map to another. Gazella Peak, for example, was also known to us as Bandersnatch. No doubt, Stejneger Peak is the official name for the mountain commonly called Tonk; somehow, after having been part of the Bird Island scene, I cannot conceive of that mighty rock, or could I ever refer to it, as anything but Tonk. My companions will forgive me for coining the name Seal Valley, which, so far as is known, occurs on no Bird Island map outside my own, but I felt obliged to help my readers locate a nameless area described by me as a valley filled with fur seals. Although my maps are based on those provided by the British Antarctic Survey, the British are in no way responsible for my selections.

My going to Bird Island the first time in 1974 was purely accidental—the result of my being unable to reach a planned destination in an entirely different region of the Southern Ocean. The unexpected adventure was also fortuitous because two years later it led to another, much longer stay on Bird Island, affording me the marvelous opportunity not only to expand

PREFACE AND ACKNOWLEDGMENTS

the scope of my Antarctic bird studies, but also to work closely with biologists of another nation. I gained much from British wisdom and field expertise.

The field study on Bird Island was made possible through prior arrangements between the United States Antarctic Research Program and the British Antarctic Survey. Dr. Robert H. Rutford, former Director, and Dr. George A. Llano, former Acting Chief Scientist, Division of Polar Programs, Washington, D. C., sanctioned my Bird Island proposal, which met the final approval of Dr. Richard M. Laws, Director, British Antarctic Survey, Cambridge, England. I also am indebted to the Government of the Falkland Islands for allowing me to visit land and sea areas under its jurisdiction; for assistance in obtaining scientific permits, I owe a debt of gratitude to Mr. D. R. Morrison, Office of the Secretariat at Stanley, and to Mr. Mick Pawley, Base Commander, Magistrate's Office, South Georgia.

My first trips to South Georgia and Bird Island in 1974 greatly influenced my decision to return there this last time, and for this I feel indebted to everyone who assisted me from the beginning. Twice during 1974, I traveled on three different ships to or from the South Georgian area: RRS *John Biscoe* under Captain E. M. S. Phelps, HMS *Endurance* under Captain Noël Bearne, and MS *Lindblad Explorer* under Captain Hasse Nilsson; in 1976, I sailed on RRS *John Biscoe* under Captain Phelps and HMS *Endurance* under Captain David L. Deakin. Many thanks to these ship's masters and their crews and passengers.

Many people assisted me in ways too numerous to mention, but special thanks go to Jean M. Parmelee, my wife; and to Ms. Diane Berube, Ms. Mary Brozic, Ms. Arlene Fosdick, Mr. Arthur E. Holt, Ms. Beverly J. Kaemmer, Mr. Robert N. Taylor, Dr. H. B. Tordoff, Mr. William A. Wood, and Mr. Walter Zambino, all of the University of Minnesota; Mr. J. Bomfiglio and Ms. Astrid Blomquist of Buenos Aires; Dr. H. Albert Hochbaum of Delta, Manitoba, Ms. Carol Masters of Minneapolis, and Dr. Olin Sewell Pettingill, Jr. of Wayne, Maine.

I am especially grateful for the times spent in the field with my British companions. For how could there be another encounter with the likes of Tony Jackson at the British base Halley Bay chiseled out of solid ice in the bowels of an Antarctic glacier? And nothing can equal the predawn climb with Julian Priddle up the snow petrel cliffs of Signy; or the first impression of South Georgia's tussock and seals on the molly slopes of Elsehul with big Al Smith; or the hike with Bob Hanks through Bore

PREFACE AND ACKNOWLEDGMENTS

Valley and up and over the snow pass to the fiords of Maiviken; or the trip to the headlands of Cooper Bay with Dave Fletcher, one of the Survey's base commanders, who epitomizes the best of his lot.

And how could I match those wild gemini boat trips with Marty Shakesby, and those pleasant days afloat with *John Biscoe*'s crew, especially Hugh Binnie, David Bray, Jerry Cutland, and Bob Wade, and my traveling companions Bill Block, Ricky Chinn, Eric Harvey, Rod Herbert, Bill Sloman, and others?

How could there be another crowning moment such as that when the likable Scot Don McKay presented me with the British Antarctic Survey medal of comradeship—a simple navy blue tie embellished with little white penguins? The tie is a mark of distinction usually reserved for those gallant Britishers who have both summered and wintered in Antarctica for two consecutive years, a unique experience I would never realize.

All this and more. Had W. Nigel Bonner, Head of the British Antarctic Survey's Life Science Division, not introduced me to Bird Island, I would not have had the pleasure of spending some of my finest hours afield with John P. Croxall, Bruce Pearson, and Peter A. Prince.

BIRD ISLAND SPECIES

Common or vernacular names for birds are fairly reliable the world over, but they fail us in far southern regions. Ones that cause a lot of confusion are "giant petrel" and "giant fulmar" when used to identify the same bird of the genus *Macronectes*. The problem is compounded by the existence of two species, a southern one called *giganteus*, and a northern one, *halli*. Seamen who do not distinguish the two call each by the name "stinker." I refer to these birds either as southern giant petrel or northern giant petrel and trust that my readers will not mistake them for the much smaller fulmars of Arctic and Antarctic regions.

Only a single species of gull breeds in far southern latitudes, but it is known by at least three English names—southern black-backed, kelp, or Dominican gull. Since the last name is generally recognized, I will use that one.

Shags are true cormorants. The names shag and cormorant are interchangeable. The one Bird Island species of duck has been called a teal, but currently it is classified as a pintail and goes by that name. One would suppose that the same reasoning would apply to the Cape pigeon, which is a petrel, but the name pigeon is the most common and widely used.

It is expedient to abbreviate long or cumbersome bird names that are used time and again. Gentoo penguins are here referred to as gentoos, wandering albatrosses as wanderers, and diving petrels as divers. The name molly, an abbreviation for mollymawk, mollymauk, or mollyhawk, is a name given certain small albatrosses. The mollies of Bird Island are the "black-brows" and "gray-heads." Light-mantled sooty albatrosses are sometimes called "sooties," but those of Bird Island should not be confused

BIRD ISLAND SPECIES

with another species, the Sooty Albatross (*Phoebetria fusca*) that breeds farther north.

Common and scientific names of Bird Island species used in this book are as follows:

King Penguin (*Aptenodytes patagonicus*)	uncommon non-breeder
Chinstrap Penguin (*Pygoscelis antarctica*)	uncommon breeder
Gentoo Penguin (*Pygoscelis papua*)	common breeder
Macaroni Penguin (*Eudyptes chrysolophus*)	common breeder
Wandering Albatross (*Diomedea exulans*)	common breeder
Black-browed Albatross (*Diomedea melanophris*)	common breeder
Gray-headed Albatross (*Diomedea chrysostoma*)	common breeder
Light-mantled Sooty Albatross (*Phoebetria palpebrata*)	common breeder
Southern Giant Petrel (*Macronectes giganteus*)	common breeder
Northern Giant Petrel (*Macronectes halli*)	common breeder
Cape Pigeon (*Daption capense*)	uncommon breeder
Snow Petrel (*Pagodroma nivea*)	uncommon, breeding unconfirmed
Antarctic Prion (*Pachyptila desolata*)	common breeder
Blue Petrel (*Halobaena caerulea*)	common breeder
White-chinned Petrel (*Procellaria aequinoctialis*)	common breeder
Wilson's Storm Petrel (*Oceanites oceanicus*)	common breeder
Black-bellied Storm Petrel (*Fregetta tropica*)	uncommon breeder
Gray-backed Storm Petrel (*Garrodia nereis*)	rare, breeding unconfirmed
South Georgia Diving Petrel (*Pelecanoides georgicus*)	common breeder
Kerguelen Diving Petrel (*Pelecanoides urinatrix*)	common breeder
Blue-eyed Shag (*Phalacrocorax atriceps*)	uncommon breeder
Yellow-billed Pintail (*Anas georgica*)	common breeder
White-rumped Sandpiper (*Calidris fuscicollis*)	rare vagrant
American Sheathbill (*Chionis alba*)	common breeder
Brown Skua (*Catharacta lonnbergi*)	common breeder
Dominican Gull (*Larus dominicanus*)	uncommon breeder
Antarctic Tern (*Sterna vittata*)	uncommon breeder
South Georgia Pipit (*Anthus antarcticus*)	common breeder

TABLE OF CONTENTS

Color Illustrations

Group 1 (follows p. 4)
Black-browed Albatross
Light-mantled Sooty Albatrosses
Gray-headed Albatrosses
Black-browed Albatrosses
Displaying male Wandering Albatross

Group 2 (follows p. 52)
Gray-headed Albatross
Light-mantled Sooty Albatross
South Georgia Pintail
Chick of South Georgia Pintail
Chick of Blue Petrel
Chick of Brown Skua

Group 3 (follows p. 84)
Southern Giant Petrel
Northern Giant Petrel
Northern Giant Petrel feasting
   on carrion
Paired South Georgian Blue-eyed Shags

Group 4 (follows p. 132)
King Penguin
Gentoo Penguin
Macaroni Penguin
Antarctic Fur Seal

Bird Island in Antarctic Waters

Bird Island as seen from RRS John Biscoe. *Snow persists on the island's highest mountain, la Roché, despite the late date of 26 December 1976. The island's most remote site, Farewell Point, lies at extreme right.*

SOUTH WITH THE FIDS

I suspect that Bird Island is a name given many places. There is, for example, a Bird Island, Minnesota, neither an island nor famous for birds, but rather a small prairie town where once was a marsh with an island inhabited by American Indians and birds. The Bird Island of this book lies south of the 50th parallel in a remote and windy region of the South Atlantic where the ocean waters are so cold that they are classified as Antarctic. It is indeed an island, and its bird life is prodigious. Fewer than 30 species of birds breed there but, as we shall see, they are special and their total numbers are overwhelming.

Sea birds have always been favorites of mine even though I grew up observing landlocked birds in Michigan's Upper Peninsula—an area far removed from the oceans. During the Second World War, I had hoped to be among those United States Marines sent to the Aleutian Islands where sea birds abound. Instead, I spent more than a year at various places in the equatorial zone of the Pacific, where within its doldrums I saw few sea birds and nary an albatross.

My first important encounter with sea birds took place when Professor George Miksch Sutton, my mentor, took me as his field assistant to Canada's frozen Baffin Island during the summer of 1953. Polar birds were not entirely unfamiliar. Sutton's earlier writings and paintings had long before instilled in me a strong attachment for far northern regions. My being afield with George Sutton profoundly influenced my decision to continue polar research. Subsequently, I found myself organizing or joining numerous expeditions to the Canadian Arctic Islands.

One might ask why of all places polar regions appeal to ornithologists, other than, that they are good places to observe sea birds. One reason is that polar environments are conducive to biological research, if only because studying comparatively simple ecological systems with few species is easier than studying complicated ones with many species, such as occur in more temperate regions.

SOUTH WITH THE FIDS

Polar birds also are attractive subjects to illustrate. They possess colors intense enough to compete with those of tropical birds, yet so subtle as to challenge any artist. The habitats of our polar models are open to the sky unshaded by many light-absorbing layers of foliage. Their beauty is highlighted by the pristine freshness of their polar surroundings.

Because of these consuming interests in the Arctic Islands for nearly twenty years, I hardly thought about other regions, including Antarctica. Not for a moment during all that time could I even imagine that one day I would be near the austral cone of the earth, on a tiny oceanic isle called Bird Island. But my thoughts drifted southwards in 1970 when newly acquired responsibilities at the University of Minnesota curtailed my activities in the Arctic. This time it was Dr. George A. Llano who greatly influenced my life by giving me the opportunity to think seriously about south polar birds. Dr. Llano was then with the Division of Polar Programs of the National Science Foundation. Under his guidance and the sponsorship of the United States Antarctic Research Program (USARP), I traveled extensively in Antarctic waters in 1973 aboard the United States Coast Guard Cutter *Glacier* and USARP Research Vessel *Hero*. At sea I made numerous observations of birds, and when we sailed close to land, I searched for suitable breeding grounds with future sea bird studies in mind. In the vicinity of Palmer Station, the United States National Science Foundation base on Anvers Island west of the Antarctic Peninsula, I found my principal research area and, with my former student, Stephen J. Maxson, initiated my first detailed study of a south polar sea bird—the Antarctic tern (*Sterna vittata*).

The following year I made plans to continue the tern study while looking at opportunities for including university students on projects involving several sea birds. I particularly wanted to arrive at the Palmer breeding ground by mid-November, spring in the Southern Hemisphere, when the last of the migrants would be arriving from distant wintering grounds while the year-round resident birds prepared for a rapidly approaching egg-laying season.

But transportation to and from a polar study area is never certain and usually much delayed; no sooner had I decided on an early arrival at Palmer when I was informed that RV *Hero* could not get me there before December. All was not hopeless, however. The British Antarctic Survey's RRS *John Biscoe* would be in the vicinity of Anvers Island in early November. The British agreed to take me to Palmer, provided that ice conditions permitted reasonably safe passage. Only ten nautical miles from Palmer the *John Biscoe* pushed sluggishly through a sea of ice, faltered,

4

Black-browed Albatross high above the Bird Sound that
separates Bird Island from South Georgia in far background.
Photographed 11 December 1976.

Light-mantled Sooty Albatrosses in the vicinity of Cobbler's
Mound. Looking eastward across Bird Sound to South Georgia.
Photographed 26 November 1976.

Gray-headed Albatrosses cavorting before Bird Island's prominent peaks—Molly Hill (middle foreground), Tonk (left), and la Roché (right). Photographed 7 December 1976.

Black-browed Albatrosses at cliff site. Photographed during author's brief landing at Elsehul, South Georgia on 14 December 1974.

Displaying male Wandering Albatross reaching skyward with his nearly eleven foot (3.35 meters) wing span. Photographed 19 December 1976.

Cape pigeon.

then lay dead in the water. Several times thereafter it inched forward, but it was apparent that we were not going farther.

William Sloman of the British Antarctic Survey told me that the ship's master had wisely decided to turn back. The vessel maneuvered slowly around and retreated along a trail of broken ice. It was a bitter disappointment, but there was nothing for me to do but study my remaining options: Either I debark *John Biscoe* in the Falkland Islands at Stanley, our next port of call, and there await uncertain passage south to Palmer, or I remain aboard and sail eastward with the British to South Georgia and other islands in the South Atlantic.

My decision was immediate. I had read Robert Cushman Murphy's eulogies on South Atlantic sea birds following his 1912-13 expedition aboard the whaling brig *Daisy*; what ornithologist in his right mind would turn down a trip to South Georgia?

Aboard *John Biscoe* were many scientists and support personnel, all of whom customarily are called "Fids," an acronym for Falkland Island Dependencies Survey. It was the Fids who, in putting me ashore at various bays and headlands, introduced me to the incredible tussock that pervades the islands of the South Georgian group—which I have a natural inclination to call "the tussock isles."

CHAPTER 2

King Edward Cove, South Georgia. The defunct whaling station, old Grytviken, lies in ruin across the waters that once turned red from the blood of whales. RRS John Biscoe *rests at the edge of new Grytviken, the British Antarctic Survey base. In the foreground Shackleton House rises high to memorialize Great Britain's polar explorer. Photographed 24 November 1974.*

TUSSOCK ISLES

As long ago as 1775, while exploring and searching for the mysterious and elusive southern continent thought in his day to be a rich and hospitable land, Captain James Cook looked upon Bird Island and named it "Bird Isle . . . on account of the vast number (of birds) that were upon it." The little isle less than six kilometers long did not take up much of his time, for he surmised that the larger land close by was the long sought-after Terra Australis Incognita.

But the larger land proved to be only 170 kilometers long and for the most part less than 40 kilometers wide—merely another uninhabited island. Captain Cook honored his king by naming it South Georgia. Some historians believe that the island may have been seen as early as 1502 by the Italian explorer Amerigo Vespucci. A stronger case has been made for the English explorer Antonio de la Roché, who reputedly viewed the island in 1675. Recognition for the discovery of South Georgia nevertheless rests with Captain Cook, because it was he who charted the island's coasts, landed, and claimed the land for Great Britain through formal declaration.

South Georgia's early discovery has greater impact when one realizes that the island appears on the map as a minuscule dot, far from any continental land mass. Lying in a great ocean some 1,740 kilometers east of the lower tip of South America, at approximate latitudes 53-55° (Welcome Islands most northerly 53°57'; First Rock most southerly 54°56') and longitudes 35-39° (Filchner Rocks most easterly 35°43'; Ramp Rock most westerly 38°18'), South Georgia shapes part of an underwater mountain range that begins in the Chilean Andes and ends in the mountains of Antarctica.

If it were possible to drain the ocean basin of this great Southern Ocean, one would see a long submarine mountain range extending eastward from the southern end of South America. Far out in the immense basin the range turns southeast, then arcs sharply back towards the west. Eventually it turns southwest and joins the Antarctic Peninsula. This out-

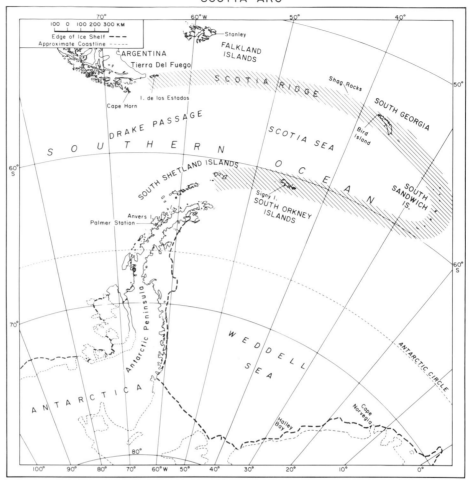

stretched ridge of mountains forms the Scotia Arc; waters within its loop create the Scotia Sea.

At the sea levels seen today, the Scotia Arc is underwater except at a few places where the tips of its highest mountains emerge as oceanic islands. If we start at the Tierra del Fuego end of the arc, Argentina's Isla de los Estados appears first. Then for many kilometers east, the arc remains deeply submerged until several mountains display their peaks modestly above water at a little-known place called Shag Rocks. Loftier mountains pushing out of the sea a full sailing day southeast of the rocks belong to the South Georgian group that includes Bird Island.

Near the apex of the arc, other high mountains pierce the waters at a number of places along a vocanically active archipelago—the South Sandwich Islands. Westward along the arc is an impressive but more austere group of islands called the South Orkneys, which lie between the Scotia Sea to the north and Weddell Sea to the south. As one approaches the spectacularly rugged Antarctic Peninsula, a long string of islands come into view, the South Shetlands. They are noticeably colder and more barren, and the largest among them are heavily weighted with glacial ice sheets.

The rich vegetation of Bird Island. Bull fur seal high in North Valley. Photographed 28 November 1976.

South Georgia and Bird Island are more hospitable, endowed with a richer flora and fauna; because of these characteristics, in addition to their low latitudinal position, they are categorized as Sub-Antarctic. Some scientists insist, however, that a better standard for judgment on these matters is the islands' position relative to that of the Antarctic Convergence.

People sailing the southern seas soon become aware of the convergence because, even though invisible, it is a good topic for conversation. The convergence is real enough and in many respects is a well-defined boundary. It occurs wherever cold surface waters flowing northward from Antarctica suddenly come up against warmer waters flowing southward.

Waters on opposite sides of the convergence differ in more than temperature. The southern Antarctic waters are heavier, contain more oxygen and nutrients, and accommodate an animal fauna distinct from that of the northern Sub-Antarctic waters. The two waters do not mix readily, the heavier ones sinking below the lighter. Animals unaccustomed to abrupt changes in temperature immediately succumb to stress at the convergence, where predatory birds easily harvest the sick krill and other small animals.

Enormous numbers of sea birds congregate and feed at the conver-

9

gence. I have seen such concentrations, but not every time during my many crossings. When sea birds fail to indicate the location of the convergence, one relies on the ship's crew, who quickly find the boundary with thermometers.

The convergence forms a continuous line all around Antarctica; all waters south of it are often referred to as the Southern Ocean. It is not an even line that runs at the same parallel but rather an undulating one that swings north and south at varying distances from the icy continent. It drifts uncommonly far north into the South Atlantic so that South Georgia and Bird Island lie 350 kilometers south of it. Consequently scientists classify those islands surrounded by cold water as Antarctic rather than Sub-Antarctic.

Nevertheless, some scientists argue that the South Georgian region is distinctly Sub-Antarctic not only because of its luxuriant flora but also because of certain faunal forms usually associated with the northern zone. Indeed, a strange biological mixture is present, representative of southern and northern zones. My British colleagues, who have a talent for cutting words to a minimum when going to the heart of an argument, say simply that South Georgia has all that Antarctica has . . . and a lot more!

South Georgia is a long, narrow, somewhat crescent-shaped island. Its long axis lies northwest to southeast, directly in the path of the fierce, nearly incessant westerly winds that roar across the Southern Ocean; the winds create turbulent air and water conditions that not only favor sea bird flight but also provide unusually good feeding grounds because of upwellings in the ocean waters. These nutrient-rich upwellings provide the basis for an extraordinarily productive food chain. At the lower end of the chain are miscroscopic, one-celled plants.

Feeding on these diatoms and other small plants are vast numbers of miscroscopic animals that in turn provide nourishment for still larger animals—crustaccans and fishes of various kinds. Farther up the food chain, the variety and total numbers of predatory animals decrease, until at the top are relatively few predators—the sea birds, seals, and whales.

South Georgia is far more rugged than I had anticipated. From aboard ship, its many glaciated mountains appear to rise straight out of a tumultuous, iceberg-studded sea. Their snowy peaks, partly obscured by rings of white and purplish clouds, attain heights of 2,950 meters elevation. When one approaches the land closely, however, broad valleys and small alluvial plains appear, dispelling impressions of a totally inhospitable land.

Summer snow lines extend 600 meters high in places along the island's warmer north coast, which supports several hundred species of plants, mostly mosses and lichens but also a handful of vascular plants, among

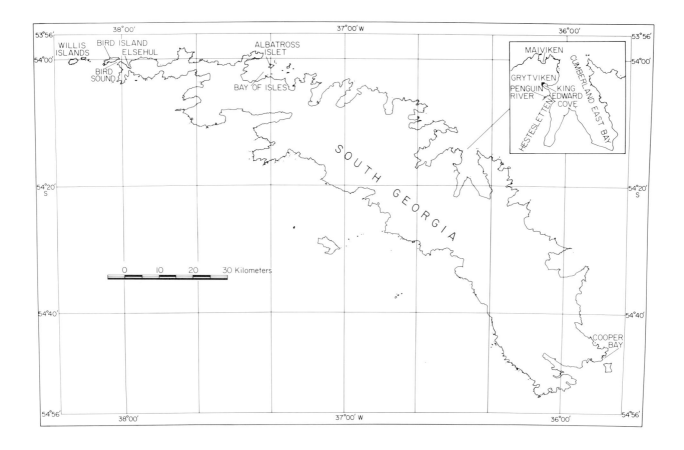

them a small flowering Antarctic buttercup (*Ranuculus biternatus*). Although the climax vegetation is grass heath, South Georgia's most striking plant is a strange tussock grass (*Poa flabellata*) that grows profusely from near the edge of the sea to well over 250 meters elevation on mountain slopes.

Tussock is ankle to knee deep in many places, but in certain areas it rises like a forest reaching one's chest, or even, as on Bird Island, above one's head. About this special plant I shall have much to say, for its influence on man and beast is so great in these oceanic lands that I always think of them as tussock isles.

A sprinkling of small tussock isles embellishes the coasts of South Georgia. Bird Island is one of them. At approximately 54°00′S and 38°03′W, the island lies a short distance off the western tip of South Georgia, though separated by a ribbon of unfriendly water called Bird Sound. One navigates the sound's rocky and kelp-choked waters to reach Bird Island's few landing beaches. More often than not the surf at these

11

beaches is too heavy for safe boat landings. All other approaches are blocked by sea cliffs, including spectacular ones along the isle's seaward side.

Exploitation of Bird Island's wildlife has been mercifully neglected. The isle's peculiar isolation doubtless has kept commercial hunters from readily landing on its shores in quest of birds and seals. To understand the animal life of present-day Bird Island, however, we first must consider important events that shaped South Georgia's romantic but bloody history.

Historic records inform us that after Captain Cook's account of the region's animal wealth, commercial hunters arrived at South Georgia in the late 1700s and early 1800s from many places, including North America. The slaughter of seals that followed would be incomprehensible to conservation-sensitive persons today. By 1830 man had nearly exterminated the Antarctic fur seal (*Arctocephalus tropicalis gazella*) at South Georgia and other islands of the Scotia Arc.

Owing to a rapid deterioration of the fur seal industry, the sealers concentrated next on the southern elephant seal (*Mirounga leonina*). Its slaughter was no less ferocious, and by 1865 its business all but finished.

The whaling industry got off to a slow start. Why bother with whales when profitable seals in the beginning were easily harvested? Besides, methods for catching and killing whales were so primitive at the time that whalers chased only the small species and passed up the large, unmanageable ones.

When a glutted Chinese market no longer required seal skins, the hunters replaced rowboats and hand-held harpoons with steam-driven whale catchers that carried sophisticated harpoon guns mounted on their bows. At the turn of the century, these modern weapons announced the beginning of the end for whales.

All whales, large and small, were hauled to shore stations that sprang up in several places on South Georgia. By 1904 a Norwegian sea captain founded the island's best-known station, Grytviken, at a harbor called King Edward Cove. The latter, itself called Grytviken before the name later came to be transferred to the whaling station, occupies one of the inner confinements of Cumberland East Bay — a deep indentation of South Georgia's north coast. Although businessmen from Buenos Aires financed the Grytviken venture, indicating an early Argentine interest in the area, the Argentinian claim to South Georgia is based mostly on the Papal Bull of 1493 dividing South America between Spain and Portugal. For many years, however, down to the present the island has remained part of the Falkland Island Dependencies. The British Antarctic Survey currently occupies South Georgia, but the island is administered by the Falklands.

Today Grytviken lies in ruin. Vacated houses, stores, administrative buildings, a church, a foundry, a great reservoir with a small hydroelectric plant, even a fleet of badly listing or submerged whale catchers, all nestle beside rushing streams at the foot of gorgeous snowy mountains. The size of the whaling factories, the immenseness of the rendering pots and other devices for processing the whales give some idea of the killing that took place. The waters of King Edward Cove turned red with blood, according to old accounts, during the height of the shore-based operations between 1910 and 1930. Little wonder that by 1965 the whale stocks crashed, and with them, Grytviken's industry.

The only occupied year-round facility on South Georgia these days is a British Antarctic Survey base located on a point of land in King Edward Cove directly across from Grytviken. The site was used in 1925 as a marine biological station concerned with whale research, but by 1969 the British Antarctic Survey had introduced a multidisciplinary approach in the biological and physical sciences. Today the base's physical plant is an aggregation of buildings. The most pretentious is one equipped with modern scientific laboratories and called Shackleton House memorializing Great Britain's polar explorer. The base itself has recently acquired the name Grytviken, though it should not be confused with the disused whaling station.

Not much can be done for the defunct whaling industry of South Georgia. But though the desecration of whales is discouraging, the seals that suffered a comparable setback have made a notable comeback. Elephant seals now carpet the bone-strewn beaches of King Edward Cove. These enormous one-to-three ton creatures occupy open areas between the buildings of the occupied British base and clutter the roads and foot-paths to Shackleton House. Antarctic fur seals appear to be increasing rapidly over most of their range as well.

Fur seals were nearly nonexistent on South Georgia only twenty-eight years ago when Niall Rankin (1951) published his splendid book on the wildlife of that island. Rankin considered those mammals to be South Georgia's greatest animal rarity and did not divulge the location of their few remaining retreats.

Although Rankin sailed extensively around South Georgia in his expedition boat, he was not able to make more than one brief landing on Bird Island. If the island had fur seals then, he does not say so. Presumably isolated pockets of them existed, for there is reason to believe that Bird Island lies at the focal point of a current fur seal explosion.

The contrast between Rankin's time and the present is striking. His was a period when whales were still being hauled to shore-based stations, and seals were dangerously scarce. Today, virtually no whales remain in those once celebrated hunting waters off South Georgia, but seals overflow the beaches—upwards of eighty thousand fur seals on tiny Bird Island!

I did not fully appreciate the extent of the fur seal comeback until I set foot on Bird Island. But like Niall Rankin before me, I soon appreciated the difficulties of going ashore by boat—even by modern rubber boats designed for tricky beach landings and called "gemini" by the British and "zodiacs" by Americans. While still aboard *John Biscoe* in 1974, the one opportunity I had to go ashore with the Fids by gemini was foiled by the persistently high winds that have long distinguished the region.

Unlike poor Rankin, I had at my means not only gemini but also twin helicopters from the British naval ice patrol and hydrographic vessel, HMS *Endurance*. Because of these helicopters I finally landed on Bird Island.

Before departing South Georgia I transferred from the *John Biscoe* to *Endurance* in company with Nigel Bonner of the British Antarctic Survey. Through many years' experience on South Georgia, Bonner developed a keen knowledge of the area's wildlife, wrote an enduring treatise on fur seals, and has the distinction of being the first scientist to camp on Bird Island both with a companion and alone. This day he had arranged to have the ship's helicopters drop him off at remote places when we sailed near South Georgia, and he invited me to go along. At Bird Island we had three precious hours.

A tidal wave of fur seals fanned out in all directions when the helicopter dipped down to sea level and put us off near several wooden huts not far from the beach. The hordes returned almost immediately when the noisy chopper flew off.

Nigel was none too happy with the landing. He momentarily complained about the incompatibility of seals and helicopters then dashed over to Lönnberg House, by far the largest of four huts, and returned with two wooden poles. He handed me one and said that it was essential to carry a club at all times on Bird Island. Then he showed me how to use it.

He did not have to go far to demonstrate. By then hundreds of seals surrounded us, among them big harem bulls with nasty dispositions. Gentle taps on the snouts kept them at bay.

No scientists were on Bird Island that year and the buildings were nailed shut. Lönnberg House had been named for the naturalist who participated in the 1901-1903 Swedish Antarctic Expedition to South Georgia. The sumptuous hut had been erected in the early 1960s by the United States Antarctic Research Program. The round USARP insignia remains intact above its heavy door.

That day, December 2, 1974, I saw more seals during a three-hour period than I had seen in a lifetime. And nowhere had I seen anything in the bird world like the sights that unfolded before me on the tussocky slopes of Bird Island. By the time the helicopter returned for us, I was making plans for a return trip.

Twenty-two months later I was back at Lönnberg House.

Lönnberg House nestles among the many seals ringing Jordan Cove. Beyond the cove lies Square Pond peninsula. The summit of Molly Hill appears in the far background. Photographed 19 November 1976.

CHAPTER 3

A huge elephant seal challenges the Fids as they roll the heavy diesel drum up a watery pathway to Lönnberg House. Wielding a bamboo pole, John Croxall clears the way for Bruce Pearson (center) and Peter Prince. Photographed by the author the day of his arrival at Bird Island on 14 November 1976.

LÖNNBERG HOUSE: THE FIRST NIGHT

As Robert Burns knew, "The best laid schemes of mice and men gang aft a-gley." All the precautions I took to ensure my being put on the first British ship to Bird Island in October 1976 were in vain.

I added an additional week to cover the usual delays inevitable in travelling south. Not good enough! My reserved seat on the once-a-week flight from Comodoro Rividavia, Argentina, to Stanley in the Falkland Islands was commandeered along with several others, by a group of Argentine VIPs. To add to my difficulties, *John Biscoe*'s arrival and departure appointments had been stepped up a week. By the time I landed at Stanley's airport, she had departed for South Georgia and Bird Island.

My only recourse was to lay new plans and salvage the waiting time until *John Biscoe* returned to the Falklands. Paraguayan snipes (*Capella gallinago magellanica*) in the wet pastures of Stanley and elusive rufous-breasted dotterels (*Zonibyx modestus*) on its coastal hills of diddle-dee took up the extra time, for these little known shorebirds warranted study, however brief.

John Biscoe did not remain long in South Georgia. On 2 November she returned to Stanley on a good wind and sea and promptly departed with me aboard for an obscure island near the Antarctic Peninsula. After some routine shore operations, my old friend Captain Phelps set *John Biscoe* on a direct course for South Georgia. Bird Island was his first scheduled stop. My luck had turned around; with it, my thoughts for a season that was still very much alive.

"November 14, Southern Ocean, enroute to Bird Island, aspect foggy, sea fairly rough, more birds than usual" was entered in my daily log on the eve of debarkation. That day I experienced an excitement known mostly to youth. All the good moments afield that I had experienced passed through my thoughts. I knew that great things were ahead.

I remember clearly making the hourly bird counts from both stern and bow, meditating on my equipment, packing and repacking the duffle bags, discovering that I had taken the wrong camera lens. And I remember the clutching fear that the promised landing on Bird Island somehow would be aborted. Then I got caught up in the business of photographing the ever-increasing numbers of Cape pigeons that drifted by on wind currents alongside the ship.

When we were midway through lunch, several small islands loomed up in the fog—the Willis Islands, and just beyond, Bird Island. All the frustration of several weeks vanished. Streams of Cape pigeons kept circling our ship. An immense flock numbering into the hundreds alighted on the waters nearby when the anchor dropped at 13:30 hours.

Many giant petrels flew by, mostly the northern species called *halli*, but what caught my eye were the fifty or more white-chinned petrels lifting off the waters far to port. Until then I had never seen a flock of them at sea. These large black petrels with nearly indiscernible white throat patches have long been called "shoemakers" by European seamen because these birds that vocalize much of the time in their nesting burrows evidently remind the sailors of their home-town cobblers who, while working in their little shoe shops, sing often. At sea the birds are often singly or in widely scattered twos and threes.

John Biscoe in approaching Bird Island from the south had entered a smooth stretch of sea near Bird Sound. These were dangerous and not very navigable narrows that separated Bird Island from the much larger South Georgia. The waters we finally anchored in were hospitable enough, though the fog that worsened hourly disturbed me. Captain Phelps assured me that it was the condition of the surf that mattered, not the fog.

Fog did not concern him or his crew, despite the presence of many ominous icebergs. At such times, one relies on those who know their electronic equipment. So, when our first mate, Andy Baker, ordered the lowering of two gemini and a much larger wooden launch, I sighed with relief, quickly gathered my gear, and stood by awaiting my orders. Only then was I reassured.

First to depart were the gemini laden with supplies and several crewmen eager to go ashore. Powered by huge outboard engines, the gemini fairly skipped along the flat surface and soon disappeared in the fog that now enveloped much of Bird Island. Their straight course indicated that the first mate knew exactly where he was going. A short time later we followed in the launch.

The less than kilometer-long trip proved uneventful. A stray snow petrel circled above us, and I saw a few penguins porpoising off our port and starboard sides. A seal popped its head out of the unusually calm waters as we entered a small inlet that I later discovered was Jordan Cove.

White-chinned petrel.

LÖNNBERG HOUSE: THE FIRST NIGHT

Before us, the gemini maneuvered. Beyond them, as far as one could penetrate the fog up and down the pebbly beaches, were squirming masses of seals, seemingly concerned only with dominance and territoriality.

A sharp voice from shore called out my name as our boat sped toward the beach. At once I recognized Peter Prince, then John Croxall, both of whom I had met six months earlier at the British Antarctic Survey headquarters in Cambridge, England. Peter and John were to be my Bird Island companions, along with a third Fid I had not seen before, Bruce Pearson. Bruce, a tall, athletic person, was a professional artist and photographer. Under the influence and schooling of Peter Prince, whom he had assisted daily for several seasons on Bird Island, Bruce became familiar with the island's wildlife.

The waters in the cove remained calm as the fog thickened. The first mate bellowed orders to depart about the time Peter, John, and Bruce began rolling heavy fuel drums up a shallow stream toward Lönnberg House. Suddenly an enormous elephant seal towered above them and lunged. The beast must have absorbed my every thought, for even now I cannot for the life of me remember photographing the foursome. I am still astonished at having found the picture months later while reviewing films in the comforts of my Minnesota home.

As we made our way slowly up the stream bed, lunging seals came at us from all sides. Most were vicious fur seals. Even though a big bull fur seal weighs considerably less than even an average-sized elephant seal, it is more aggressive and downright dangerous. Wielding a bamboo pole impressively, one of my British companions moved the seals out while the rest of us rolled the drums in. At Lönnberg House we chased several seals off the porch and ducked inside. Though mentally fatigued, I was exuberant at having finally reached Bird Island, and I felt much at home.

Milling masses of seals barked incessantly. Scattered among them were penguins, skuas, pintail ducks, giant petrels, and what seemed to me extraordinary numbers of sheathbills. The latter, white-plumaged and chickenlike in size and form, ran close behind newly born seal pups and with sharp parrotlike bills snipped off the trailing umbilical cords. Nothing edible goes begging around Lönnberg House.

By then the fog was so dense that the tussock hills surrounding the inlet were invisible. Later, I knew these prominences were dotted with white specks—nesting albatrosses, no less, and all looked down on little Lönnberg House in its world of seals.

First impressions are best. Inside the cluttered quarters of Lönnberg House I sensed immediately that this was a scientific laboratory, not merely a refuge in the wilderness.

LÖNNBERG HOUSE: THE FIRST NIGHT

Exploratory field work breaks down two ways. The first or "romantic" kind requires physical prowess; human strength and ingenuity are pitted against the elements. The more inhospitable the environment, the better to test one's endurance. This kind of exploration calls for physical and mental achievement under the most trying conditions: the climbing of an unscalable peak, the crossing of a crevassed ice sheet, a solo flight into the unknown. This is field adventure that thrills the hearts of millions.

In the literature of these special people, much of the writing is devoted to the weather, especially cold, wind, and precipitation, and to special clothing and food caches that include the precise stores of a few important foods. Endurance above all is essential to achieving the usual single objective, often a distant, hard-to-reach place.

The second type of exploratory field work is quite different. These field workers cram as many worldly goods as humanly possible into their tents, or better still, their heated wooden huts, and write blessed little about their equipment and stores. The more comfortable and equipped they are, the better they cope with their varied research studies—which may thrill the hearts of few.

The objectives of these people are not concerned with physical endurance, although the all-consuming hours that go into their work attest to a kind of academic endurance. For my British colleagues at Lönnberg House, the objectives are clear—seek and study the lives of birds and seals in a meaningful but practical way.

One glance tells it all: benches full of scientific equipment and notebooks; shelves stacked with books, reprints, and card files; dry socks and boots hanging from the ceiling above a coal-burning range equipped with a vat for hot water and a baking oven; electric light bulbs wired to a portable generator housed in a shack nearby. And incredibly, considering the primitive state of Bird Island, a system of plumbing that started with a long rubber hose at a nearby waterfall and ended in a store-bought sink with a water faucet.

Amid this luxury one fact was paramount: Immediately outside the hut's thirteen windows was the wildest scene conceivable—wildlife to top an eight-ring circus. Going full tilt day and night seven days a week was a tumult of screaming, rocking, throbbing, lunging bodies large and small, seemingly intermeshed and intermingled. Within arm's reach.

For a long time I stood at the back window and watched troop after troop of gentoo penguins waddling up one of the stony creeks to a roost that grew steadily in size as the light dimmed in the ever-thickening fog.

Peter Prince cooked a special dinner that night—fresh lamb ribs pulled from a crude deep freeze set up near the generator. A deep freeze. Imagine! I was so taken with the lean but delicious ribs that Peter called

The crowded seal beaches of Bird Island. Photographed near Lönnberg House on 8 December 1976.

Stanley greyhounds that I forgot to record the rest of the fare. No doubt it was canned potatoes, stewed tomatoes, boiled peas, and a crusty dessert. The special ribs were so named because they are acquired at Port Stanley in the Falklands, and because like greyhounds, they are long and lean.

The good food, extra-fine sherry, and comfortably warm room, topping a day jam-packed with excitement, did me in. Despite the rock music that blared from a cassette above Peter's work bench, I had to struggle to stay awake. On few occasions had I ever been so tired as at that moment when all hell broke loose at Lönnberg House.

It started with a thump on a window pane. Peter ran outside, flashlight in hand, and disappeared in the fog. John rushed to the window; he shouted back over his shoulder that one of the camp skuas had caught a prion and was plucking it alive.

Peter snatched the prion from the skua and brought it inside. The delicate, bluish-gray petrel had lost a good many feathers, but was otherwise unharmed. Peter gently stuffed it in a cloth sack for the time being and ran out again, leaving the porch door wide open.

More thuds. Then scores of them. Birds were crashing into the windows; birds were coming inside the hut through the open door. Outside, the air was teeming with birds, the ground crawling with them.

I followed John and Bruce outside but remained on the porch, fearing to go further lest I step unwittingly onto a seal. Birds flying by brushed my cheeks with their soft wings. Others crashed into my chest, and lord knows how many ran over my toes. I grabbed one that was running through the doorway, and it proved to be a blue petrel—a live blue petrel in hand. These birds usually are seen only at a distance from aboard ship, often far from land.

The men dashed about stuffing the helpless birds in cloth sacks. Flashlight beams dancing wildly picked up the eerie, ghostlike birds; everywhere shafts of light pierced the fog. Peter shouted that the diving petrels were coming; John shouted above him that he had a storm petrel.

21

LÖNNBERG HOUSE: THE FIRST NIGHT

With all the commotion, I marveled at how they avoided running headlong into the seals.

Standing on the sanctuary of the porch, I felt secure, but it was a false security: I didn't know then that the spot was favored by many a sleeping seal. With all the hubbub, the seals had retreated, if only temporarily.

The petrels kept coming. Hundreds.

The sacking of petrels slowed only when my companions became selective. Above the din of calls, thrashing wings, and thumping bodies, Peter shouted that we had enough prions but that we should take a few more blues and divers—and all the "stormies" we could catch. Obviously the skuas were enjoying a windfall, so my friends soon called a halt to the operation by closing the door securely and blocking the light that streamed from the many windows. Bruce went outside to turn off the generator and, following the blackout, the thumpings subsided.

For the next several hours the four of us weighed and measured dozens of petrels by lamplight, releasing the birds outside one at a time as the work progressed. Some things were immediately apparent to me, the newcomer. Blue petrels and two species of diving petrels were indeed common on Bird Island. The two diving petrels looked so much alike that I could not separate them in the hand, let alone in the field. Peter, on the days following, carefully pointed out minute anatomical differences in body weight, bill structure, length of certain feathers, color patterns of the legs, and so on, though he apparently had little faith in plumage color characteristics previously described for the birds. On the other hand, ecological differences, according to Peter, were pronounced, especially with respect to habitat preferences and breeding schedules.

Rarest among the booty taken that night was a gorgeous gray-backed storm petrel of the genus *Garrodia*, the first I had ever seen. Bruce carefully held its stretched wings while John photographed them with a flash camera before freeing the bird. According to Peter, the species' breeding on Bird Island was suspected but not confirmed. The finding in nearby creek beds of a dead fledgling with flight feathers still in sheath, and an abandoned egg likely belonging to this species, respectively in 1972 and 1974, was good evidence but not proof of its breeding. Though I was ever watchful for this bird, I failed to see another on Bird Island.

The next rarest of the sacked birds were two black-bellied storm petrels of a different genus, *Fregetta*. Infrequently I had seen this rather uncommon bird far at sea, but until this night it had eluded me on land and therefore was special. Black-bellies breed at least sparingly on Bird Island, where Peter on occasion had seen their eggs and chicks in tussock burrows

Bruce Pearson's "A night on Bird Island: 'The Kitchen Window'." Wilson's storm petrel (lower left), diving petrel (lower right), blue petrel (center), Antarctic prions (upper left and right).

near Lönnberg House. But like the gray-back, I failed to see another that season.

Also in the catch was a third storm petrel, the Wilson's of still a different genus, *Oceanites*. This species is the commonest and most widely dispersed storm petrel in Antarctic and Sub-Antarctic regions. It may be the most abundant sea bird in the world. Many Wilson's storm petrels winter in the Northern Hemisphere, commonly off the Atlantic Coast of the United States during our northern summer. Invariably these birds, however, return to far southern regions to breed during the austral summer. Breeding individuals frequent the screes of Bird Island's high interior, but I have found them equally abundant at low elevations wherever they find a hidden crevice under or between rocks for their single, large egg.

How long we weighed and measured birds into the early hours of the next day, I have no idea. I was numb from exhaustion; by the time I tumbled into my bunk, I felt as though I had flying petrels thumping against my skull.

My last thought that incredible first night at Lönnberg House was, "Lord, what kind of a place is this . . . what will tomorrow bring?"

CHAPTER 4

Male wandering albatross on the tussock slopes of North Valley. Photographed 9 December 1976.

TUSSOCK, WILDLIFE
AND WIND

I don't recall the time of day we woke after that wild night with the petrels. It must have been late morning Bird Island time, but my biological clock was so hopelessly awry that time had no meaning.

I do remember being the first up, and that being the case, should have stoked the fire and heated the water for tea. These were small Lönnberg House duties that I became aware of through observation and the timely advice of Peter Prince.

I also remember stumbling through the hut and out the door to find myself among many, many seals. A brown skua with a worn band on its leg ran up to within inches of my foot, cocked its head, and eyed me suspiciously. Somehow I mistook this bird for Mavis, a camp pet, but much later learned that it was Mavis' spouse, a tough old male called George. Judging by the plucked petrel carcasses strewn about, he had had a good night.

Skuas are large, brown, gull-like birds with wing quills that flash white when spread on the ground or in flight. I especially wished to compare the skuas of Bird Island with those of the Palmer Station area.

A South Georgia pintail tugging at one of our discarded Stanley greyhound ribs caught my attention. With its finely serrated bill, it nimbly picked from the bone the last bits of fat left by the skuas. Such feeding activity by a duck amused me, but at that time I had no idea how carnivorous these little Bird Island pintails are. They thrive on seal flesh.

I stood watching the pintail glean from the sheep's rib the last morsel of fat, until a big fur seal charged and chased me back to Lönnberg House where things had begun to stir. Over a brimming cup of English tea, Peter explained—as Nigel Bonner had done previously—the problems of negotiating tussock slopes and the absolute necessity of not leaving the house without a pole or ax handle.

In no uncertain terms he told me to stay off the beaches where the seals were concentrated and aggressive. Not only could a bull fur seal bite a man severely, a slight nick by a smallish yearling cow could lay one low

25

for weeks because of the hard-to-cure infections known as "seal fingers" to commercial hunters.

Peter Prince knew a lot about seals, but his first love was the study of birds, particularly blue petrels and diving petrels. Among his current interests were white-chinned petrels and the smaller albatrosses, including light-mantled sooties. He understood the topography and wildlife of Bird Island so well that it was easy to see why he was Bird Island's civilian base commander. Peter laid down the rules, and all of us survived because of them.

After we had eaten a plateful of bacon and eggs smothered in fried tomatoes, Peter dragged down from the rafters a heavy pair of leather field shoes fitted with tough, skid-proof soles. With the shoes went a pair of canvas shin guards that, according to Peter, would ward off slick tussock mud. Fastening the guards securely to the shoes was a Fid trick I never did master, so when some time later Peter offered me a more familiar pair of knee-high rubber boots called Wellingtons, I gladly accepted.

These particular Wellingtons were specially ordered. They were fitted with steel pegs on the heels and soles to prevent slipping on the tussock and were the best single piece of field equipment I possessed.

Very little conversation percolates through Lönnberg House each morning. Each of us sits deep in thought, mulling over his plan for the day. My first planned trip was to be a simple introduction to some of the island's habitats, with John Croxall as guide. As we stood outside Lönnberg House laden with packs and ax handles, John turned and succinctly gave me two choices: climb the hill or sit out my term in the hut.

The hill he referred to looked to me like a small mountain. It loomed before us but later, as we climbed, the slope became less steep, and led to a vast upper stretch of tussock known as North Valley—one of the least pretentious areas of Bird Island, but also, as I soon discovered, one of the most productive brown skua breeding grounds imaginable.

My British companions appeared to be in their late twenties, though Bruce seemed even younger. I was the old man of the group, a generation apart, and could readily understand why John questioned my ability to get up his "hill." I was about to give it a try.

John proceeded up a steep rocky stream bed and I followed, trying desperately to keep my balance on the slippery ascent. Seals were everywhere, disputing our every step. John bluffed those directly ahead with a shout or tap of his club and they scurried off. Others leered down from the tussock banks bordering each side of the creek. At one point we left the creek and crossed a fairly level area covered with seals. Bulling our

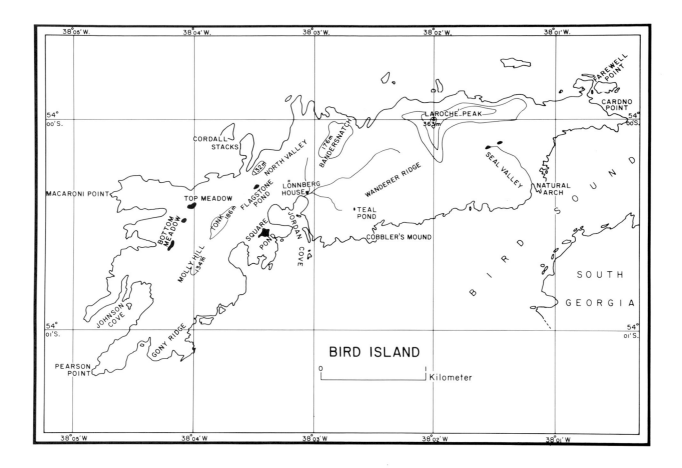

way through, we next climbed a tussock slope alive with seals. Then I had my first lesson in tussock hopping—and took my first fall.

Tussock grass grows extensively on Bird Island, from near sea level to the upper valleys, and keeps creeping up the sides of mountains in places so steep one would not dare scale them without climbing equipment. Only the summits of the island's highest mountains escape the tussock, which grows either as a continuous cover cut throughout by rills, or in scattered patches. Where the patches are widely scattered, as on rocky screes or in wet meadows, the much smaller lichens and mosses grow in the tussock-free places. A hiker looks for these openings, but on Bird Island one doesn't reach many open places without first battling jungles of tussock.

Tussock is a tough, coarse grass that grows in clumps. Old stems die, turn brown, and become soft, woody pedestals. Fresh green stems, pushing up through the old, form umbrella-shaped crowns or tufts. Tussock patches may show more green than brown, or vice versa, but during the snow-free season these contrasting colors are everywhere.

Numerous interconnecting corridors between the tussock pedestals occur wherever the grass forms a continuous cover, whether on level ground or steep slopes. Although the narrow corridors barely permit passage by man or seal, one would be tempted to use them, because the alternative is to hop from one trembling tussock crown to the next. The new-

27

comer soon discovers, however, that the tussock corridors are treacherous because—in being sheltered above by waist-high canopies of the overlapping grasses—their mud-slick, icy bottoms are hidden and all too often have drop-offs. So deceptive are these drop-offs that one risks life or limb in suddenly being pitched headlong into a deep chasm with no visible bottom. One decides to hop from clump to clump and avoid the corridors altogether.

Fur seals also prefer the high route over the tussock. In some areas their continuous movements cause widespread, severe denuding of hillsides, sometimes entire hills. The remaining scant vegetation clings to life in protected depressions around the base of each tussock pedestal. These bald hummocks, each fringed thinly with grass, reminded me of a congregation of tonsured monks.

The bare pedestals insure easy tussock hopping, except in wet weather when their smooth, peaty surfaces become dangerously slippery. During these rainy times, I cherished the cleated Wellingtons brought especially for these conditions by Peter Prince. Before long I became adept and agile in negotiating tussock slopes under a variety of conditions; but during those first days of tussock hopping, I found the going anything but fun.

A short distance up slope in North Valley we passed a prominent dome of rock mostly barren except for a tongue of enduring tussock that extended up one side. John called the dome Cave Crag and told me that on the seaward side was a cave midway up its clifflike face. During the summer months the crag is speckled with nesting black-browed albatrosses. This day, hundreds claimed the crag, and on the sheer side of a nearby mountain called Tonk, thousands. For each bird on a cliff nest, another rode the wind eddies in graceful aerodonetic displays.

At this altitude, but on more level ground, we came on the wandering albatrosses. In size alone they dwarfed their black-browed cousins. Not many adult wanderers were about this day, but many of their huge, heavy-bodied young squatted on or near nests that they had occupied for eight long months. Flowing unevenly from their dark body feathers were long strands of grayish down that shivered in the slightest breeze.

One of these dark-plumaged chicks whined piteously in front of its white-plumaged parent. The old male responded by running up to the young bird with his enormous bill agape. In placing its own enormous bill crosswise between the mandibles of its father, the hungry youngster downed a meal of regurgitated food, likely ocean squid, of which not one morsel was dropped. After the final surge of food, it continued to run its bill back and forth along the parent's lower mandible.

TUSSOCK, WILDLIFE AND WIND

I told John that I wanted to stop and photograph the feeding process. He agreed that it was a good idea because the young wanderers' flying time was fast approaching, and one by one the fledglings would slip away unnoticed. Soon the last of them would abandon the land for the sea.

An unusually bright fog low above the slope that moment favored photography. Of all the pictures I have of young wanderers being fed, the ones taken that day were best. Conditions thereafter never were as good.

The slope ahead became steeper and slipperier, the tussock and seals thinner. Here and there were bare patches of ground pockmarked by holes that John said were the nesting burrows of prions and diving petrels. The tussock thickened again, though thank heaven the seals did not, and up and over a bank to the left a gentle slope lay before us with a pretty pond called Flagstone. In its shallow but murky waters stood a dozen brown skuas. Several pintails flew off, but the skuas, after tiptoeing and dancing a little, remained.

Beyond Flagstone Pond, we approached a high, narrow pass flanked by precipitous cliffs on its north and south sides. The south cliffs drop abruptly to a wide apron of flattish, tussock-covered land with a fairly large, square-shaped and uninviting pool of black water appropriately named Square Pond. The north cliffs fall straight to the sea. From high above one can hear the pounding surf.

At the pass, which had an unusually dense population of skuas, the land tumbles gently toward the west as a great spongy meadow, known to the Fids as Top Meadow, interspersed with tussock clumps, numerous rills, and a fair-sized creek that ultimately plunges down a sea cliff. Dispersed over these pleasant meadows were many wanderers, as well as many giant petrels of the two types—the southern, or Antarctic species, and the northern, or Sub-Antarctic species.

The two species nest side by side at several places on Bird Island, but the presence of both species as breeding birds was not recognized there until 1971. According to John, the southern giant petrel had only begun to lay eggs, whereas the northern giant petrel had been setting for several weeks. The discrepancy in breeding times aids in keeping the two species apart and from interbreeding.

Their body sizes are much alike. Their plumages as well appear quite similar, though that of the southern species tends to be paler, with some individuals having nearly all white feathers. Bill colors are by far the best field characteristic. The southern species has a yellowish bill with a greenish tip, while the northern's is horn-colored with a distinctive brownish tip readily seen from a distance. Of course, I had to stop and photograph

29

the birds, paying close attention to getting both nesting species in the same frame. John, as usual, was patient. He waited as I examined the large white, heavily-stained, rather homely eggs, numbering one to a nest, also large.

No seals lived in these high meadows, but birds were plentiful. Among the wanderers, giant petrels, and skuas, we encountered many South Georgia pipits—the world's southernmost song bird, found nowhere outside this region. Even now I mentally hear the soft twittering flight songs of male pipits above the fresh meadows. Pipits of all ages flitted here and there, and at one point a stub-tailed fledgling zipped by only inches away and disappeared in the tussock. These birds were as much at ease in the tussock as they were on the ground. Grass-perching pipits! Unthinkable back home. From really dense tussock came the faint calls of hungry nestlings, but try as I might, I could not find the nest.

Walking freely over the meadows was so delightful that only when I followed John back into the tussock did I have a rude awakening. Conditions had indeed worsened. I took my second, third, and fourth tumbles and felt so clumsy that it was embarrassing. Rising ignominiously from my sprawled position, I trudged on behind my sure-footed host.

We passed a skua's nest with a single egg that John said had been laid some days before. On we went until finally we stepped onto a ridge called Macaroni Point, and what a point! Stretching before us from our lofty ridge to the sea were an estimated quarter million penguins. All macaronies, an almost unbelievable sight, with noise and stench to match.

John Croxall pointed to a detached colony of macaronies on a ridge opposite from where we stood. The much smaller colony was separated from us by a deep chasm that enclosed a fingerlike inlet where the sea's waters rushed in, boiling incessantly.

The small colony, according to John, was an ideal one to study. If I didn't mind, he would leave me now and attend to the business of weighing and measuring his marked birds. He would join me later, if not on the side of the mountain called Tonk, then back at camp.

Dr. John Croxall was a full-time biologist for the British Antarctic Survey. At the time, Bird Island was not nearly the familiar place to him that it was to Peter Prince. He had become involved only recently in albatross and penguin work, but judging from his scientific expertise, great energies, and enthusiasm for wildlife, significant contributions in sea bird biology will be forthcoming.

John's words had given me permission to roam at will, unchaperoned, which for the most part I prefer. Until then the Fids had insisted on my

being accompanied by at least one person in the event of an accident. Afterward, on Bird Island I went nearly everywhere, with few restrictions. It was, to be sure, expedient to keep off the crowded beaches, where the seals could tear one asunder, and to avoid the rims of high sea cliffs where a sudden gust of wind almost certainly would push one to eternity.

With this freedom went the responsibility of not crippling the entire Bird Island expedition with a clumsy accident. I thought about this a good deal, reminding myself of one of Professor Sutton's important rules in field biology—safety first!

The next few hours were ornithological bliss. While John wound his way down a muddy bank thickly set with albatross nests, I skirted the upper edge of the big rookery on Macaroni Point, brushing against hundreds of penguins that skittered before me over whitewashed rocks. Since few birds were on eggs, my progress was rapid.

At the far end of the ridge I sat down on a high point to take in the panoramic spectacle below. The fog lifted; the skies opened and the wind roared. More than anything else, the wind blowing across the South Georgian sea had impressed Niall Rankin. Before any of the wonderful sights of the bird and mammal world, he remembered those days when the whole

Macaroni Point with some of its quarter million macaroni penguins. Willis Islands appear in the background. Photographed 15 November 1976.

31

surface of the sea was lifted into the air and flung forward in a blinding
sheet of spindrift. Aboard ship, the wind was his crew's principal foe,
something they had to be always on the lookout for, and something that
when it did come caused the greatest disturbance in their existence.

High on the slopes of Bird Island one escapes the spindrift, but not
the teeth of the wind. It strikes with the katabatic force and suddenness
of a glacial wind, suppressing all sounds. As I stood that first time on
Macaroni Point, it was the wind, not the quarter million penguins, that I
heard most clearly.

Soon, I was forced to find shelter in the lee of the ridge, where some
of the macaronies were on eggs. My presence immediately brought in
several egg-seeking sheathbills. Even for these clever opportunists the wind
was so fierce that they were practically helpless on the wing. Whenever
one tried to land near me the wind stopped it in midair and eventually
carried it down slope. I reached up and actually touched one of the snowy-
white birds hanging prettily on the wind.

The wind slashing across the bow of Macaroni Point proved too
much, so finally I retreated along the ridge and found a sheltered tussocky
area amid incubating gray-headed and black-browed albatrosses. Their
many and peculiar pillar-shaped nests each held a bird on a single large egg.

Those wonderful creatures are so attached to their nests that they do
not flush even when one walks right by them; the intruder is not unnoticed, however, for black-brows especially have a penchant for reaching
out and giving one a painful nip. Many times I let out a yelp during my
wanderings through one of their big rookeries. There is ample evidence
that a certain anxiety exists among these albatrosses in the presence of

man, so I tried not to upset the incubating birds. I gave an especially wide berth to marked individuals being studied by my companions.

My little molly colony was in an unusually luxuriant growth of tussock on the top edge of a precipice that dropped straight to the sea many meters below. To my left this cliff took a sharp bend and continued as the north side of Macaroni Point, where, high on the cliff walls, several Cape pigeons circled.

To my right the cliff continued in a straight but rising shield of blackish rock until it, too, turned a corner and disappeared. Below the rim of its overhang flew a dainty snow petrel. Whether it actually had an egg tucked away in some hidden crevice of the crag is pure conjecture; likely no one would attempt to go down the side of that cliff to find out, even if it meant establishing a record for Bird Island.

Little molly colony perched on the eyebrow of a sea cliff. Both black-browed and gray-headed albatrosses occupy the steep tussock slope. Photographed 19 December 1976.

Far below, out of the foaming sea rose two great pillars of rock, one isolated, the other connected to Bird Island, named together the "Cordall Stacks."

Hanging precariously to the sides of these rocks were hundreds of

*Little molly colony—
another view.*

birds. Streams of gray-heads and black-brows lilted close overhead, circled back at the cliffs of Macaroni Point, then passed far below me on their return flight. I have no clear recollection how long I sat in this enchanting molly colony. The ever-changing colors and light effects on the cliffs and waters were as intriguing as those of the mollies passing in review.

I found the colors of the gray-heads especially difficult to interpret at varying distances. Close up, the birds display florid, multicolored bills against a delicate gray plumage that is somewhat fickle in appearance. At a distance, the birds' colors appear dull and uninteresting, yet at close range they are unmistakably the handsomest of the albatrosses.

Color or no color, the appearance of all these flying albatrosses is so seductive that burning up film on a windy molly ridge is a favorite Bird Island pastime. I decline to divulge how many duplicate rolls of gray-heads and black-brows ended up in my bag of photographs.

On many a subsequent trip to Macaroni Point, I found myself returning to my favorite molly colony perched on the eyebrow of a sea cliff. For long spells I would sit in awe, trying to grasp the scene before me; it surely had to be one of nature's uncomprehensible sights. By then I did, however, fully appreciate the significance of the wind and the role it played on Bird Island. Without the wind, no aerial theater.

That first day, I grudgingly pulled myself off my roost, which was an abandoned molly nest, and started back for camp, mostly because I didn't want to cause undue alarm among my companions in being late the first time out.

In a wet meadow up from the Point I came on a club of skuas, at least seventy birds in all, standing in a marshy depression crisscrossed by small streams. Like those at Flagstone Pond earlier, these skuas were disinclined to flush and did so only when I approached within a few steps. They did not fly far and returned to the same roost soon after I left.

Still higher in the tussock I came upon a white-plumaged giant petrel of the southern species, incubating complacently, though much aware of my presence. Not far away, true to form, were incubating giant petrels of the northern species.

TUSSOCK, WILDLIFE AND WIND

Up near the pass above Flagstone Pond the skuas assaulted me with screaming and dive-bombing diversions. The tempo increased to a point where I knew that I must be close to the nest of an especially aggressive pair, and, sure enough, before me in a slight mossy depression was a single brownish egg, handsomely spotted and blotched with darker browns. Braving the plunging skuas that whacked me hard several times, I carefully marked the fresh egg, and also staked the nest with a numbered wire. From that moment I began systematically to observe skuas and mark their nests.

Descending the pass into North Valley that day was no little feat. The wind drove me back so forcibly despite my steep descent that I could hardly push onward. By the time I reached the seal-infested tussock, I knew that I would have trouble trying to cope with those beasts while combating the wind. Practicing a bit of displacement behavior, as I watched the surf pounding the cove where we had landed less than 24 hours earlier, I considered that had the trip in from *John Biscoe* been delayed a few hours, I likely would still be aboard ship.

Those thoughts somehow got me over the slippery tussocks and through the ring of seals. I staggered down the slopes and rocky streamlets, bumbling and pitching most of the way, doing my best to hang on to a packsack that billowed like a gusty sail.

The seals, scores of them, didn't seem to mind the wind at all. They attacked from all sides while I sidestepped, leaped, and swung my club. The relief I felt on reaching Lönnberg House was indescribable.

Inside the hut's comfortable quarters, I found all three of my fellow inhabitants. Peter and Bruce had been to one of their special molly colonies. John had much to say about his macaronies, though I was so completely spent that what he said didn't make much sense. I scarcely recall what took place. After a day of climbing tussock one loses no sleep at night—no matter how close and vociferous the wildlife.

That evening, I vaguely remember eating dinner, then fighting a losing battle with my daily field notes, and hoping above all that we would not have another petrel night, though Peter repeatedly assured me that we would not. According to him, invasions of the sort we had experienced are rare in spring; almost invariably they occur during the post-breeding season when the young of the year are flying. He insisted that last night's invasion was atypical. We wouldn't have another very soon.

Still, Peter was not entirely correct. While rummaging about at his end of the building, he accidentally kicked one of his Wellingtons, and from the burrowlike opening of the rubber boot popped a blue petrel.

CHAPTER 5

*Blue Petrel Patch. Hidden burrows of blue petrels, Antarctic prions
and Kerguelen diving petrels riddle the ground beneath the dense tussock.
Photographed 18 November 1976.*

BLUE PETRELS

The blue petrel was the bird I most wanted to see on its breeding ground. I had observed it often enough at sea flying erratically above the turbulent waters of the Drake Passage south of Cape Horn, but I had never seen a living one close up. I had no special purpose in singling it out, but for some reason the bird holds a fascination for me. Certain birds are like that, though I do not know why.

Peter Prince is the world's authority on blue petrels. He told me that they breed early on Bird Island and that probably many were on eggs that moment. That was all it took to send me on to Pearson Point—a rugged peninsula of tussock ridges, ravines, and sea cliffs forming the southwest tip of the island—where Peter had actually camped for long periods among the blues.

Pearson Point is not difficult to reach by coastal routes when the seals are not crowding the beaches in large numbers. Since seal populations were close to peaking at the time, I had to go overland. The route suggested by Peter seemed simple, though he alerted me to certain valleys grown up to dense tussock that should be avoided because they took a person's energy and time.

I attempted my first overland hike to Pearson Point during my second day on Bird Island. The trip got off to a bad start. The wind had subsided, but fog had settled in all around by the time I made it to the top of North Valley and headed west through the narrow pass. The fog was so thick that even the mountain Tonk was obscured. Although I didn't have my only familiar landmark, I went on, thinking that eventually I would find the way.

Besides, I knew precisely where I was. Even though Macaroni Point was shrouded in fog, the telltale noise and stench from the big penguin rookery gave me my bearings. I headed in what seemed the logical direction to Pearson Point.

Along the way, I flushed several pintails from a large pond whose bank suited a nesting pair of dive-bombing skuas. After marking the two skua eggs, I climbed a nearby ridge with tussock so dense that it blocked my every move. Then I entered an almost impassable valley—a quagmire of tussock, hidden streams, and drop-offs. This surely had to be Peter Prince's tough stretch of tussock where the grass grew higher than one's head.

By the time I freed myself from that nearly inextricable mess, I was more mentally than physically exhausted. Feeling much akin to J.R.R. Tolkien's Frodo, I next found myself skirting nests of black-browed albatrosses on a steep but negotiable bank of tussock. In working my way down through the closely spaced birds, I eventually found the going much better and assured myself that I was well on my way to Pearson Point.

Then the stench and noise hit me full force. I was back at my starting point, near Macaroni Point! With no help from the fogged-in Tonk, I had made a full circle. The trip to Pearson Point would have to be put off. Since the penguin colony had beckoned twice today, I decided to see what it offered. But somehow I missed the trail leading to Macaroni Point and instead came to the edge of another molly colony composed of many grayheads and a few black-brows. It was situated on a nameless ridge across the narrow gorgelike inlet from Macaroni Point. Farther along this ridge was the separate little colony of macaronies that was being studied by my companions.

Through breaks in the fog I could just see their orange jackets ahead. In a minute, I recognized John Croxall and Bruce Pearson; they were weighing and measuring marked individuals of the penguin flock. Both greeted me enthusiastically and invited me to have lunch with them. As we sat in the tussocks sipping coffee and munching chocolate, two very curious immature fur seals moved in so close to us that Bruce finally jumped up and chased them off.

John pointed out a fine growth of tussock that extended from the cliff edge of the inlet all the way to the little molly colony I had just come through. According to him that tussock was prime habitat for the Kerguelen diving petrel—the species I had seen for the first time only two evenings before at Lönnberg House.

I was so eager to see more of these birds that I gulped my coffee and went into the tussock where in no time at all I came up with an egg hidden in a burrow at the foot of a tussock pedestal. Judging by its size, it could only have belonged to a diver. The egg was fresh and appeared to have been abandoned for some time at the burrow's entrance. I searched further and discovered that the narrow tunnel was partially filled with water. Excessive flooding must have caused the aborted nesting.

I investigated several more burrows and found nothing. The burrows themselves I found intriguing and could not resist probing them with my fingers. For the most part, they extended less than a meter into a compact

mass of tussock remains that was soft and reminded me of shredded inner bark. The pulpy material was brownish yellow, terribly cold and clammy. I noticed that it stained my hands indelibly.

Peter Prince had described the probing of petrel burrows as hellish business. As my hands and wrists quickly became numb with cold, I had to agree. The thrill of discovering the contents of a petrel's burrow is, however, worth the annoyance.

The burrow of the Kerguelen diving petrel seldom goes straight to the egg chamber; most have, as I later discovered, a twist or sharp bend. Around such a bend, in one of the more typical burrows, I touched a pulsating diver. Grasping its bill firmly, I was able to remove it harmlessly from the chamber, which held a single egg so thoroughly stained by tussock juice that one could scarcely tell that the shell was intrinsically white.

The nicest aspect of rummaging about in tussock burrows is that, if one is careful, essentially no damage is done to the burrow. Thus, I had no compunction whatever about extending my arm full length into many of the clammy passageways. I skipped the very deep ones that required excavation.

After finding the first incubating diver so easily, I thought surely I would find many more. In finding no more, I moved to another area farther along the slope below the albatross colony. At the level where the mollies, on leaving their nests, swoop down low over the tussock and close to one's head, I started to find many burrows. Since some of them were fairly large, I decided that they likely were of prion origin.

It was much too early in the season for incubating prions. I was certain of this because only the day before I had discussed with Peter the breeding schedules of a number of Bird Island species. I could not resist examining them and eventually found in one an egg that seemed much too large for either diver or prion.

Wedging my shoulder against the burrow entrance, I probed further, until I felt the sharp cutting edge of a petrel bill in a side pocket of the egg chamber. Straining still further, I got hold of that bill and slowly but surely eased from the burrow a struggling blue petrel. Few birding experiences have given me so much satisfaction.

My joy was shared by John and Bruce, who had no idea that blue petrels were breeding anywhere in the vicinity. Peter was ecstatic over the find, because for him the distance between Lönnberg House and a blue petrel colony was reduced by half. Overland trips no longer were necessary along the worst part of the trail leading to Pearson Point.

Blue petrels are not known to many people, except perhaps bird enthusiasts who sail the Southern Ocean. They often confuse the beginner because they closely resemble the prions in size, shape, and plumage. That there are several species of prions that all look alike hardly simplifies matters.

Fortunately for even the experienced observer, the blue petrel displays a conspicuous white-tipped tail that can be seen from far off. This particular characteristic makes at-sea observations of this bird quite easy, for the white tip is not present in any of the prions or other petrels.

Despite outward appearances, blue petrels are not closely related to prions. They belong to a special assemblage of procellariids known as gadfly petrels that fly with their rather short wings bent at the wrist instead of extended at full length. This anatomical difference may be the reason their flapping and gliding flight seems to be more erratic than those of shearwaters and most other petrels; and may be why they resemble prions, also highly erratic flyers.

Another gadfly characteristic is a narrow but very strong, black, hooked bill efficient for catching squid and crustaceans. The blue petrel has such a bill, and while probing the hidden corners of a burrow I quickly learned to distinguish it from the broader, considerably softer bill of the Antarctic prion. The blues latch onto a finger tip rather painfully, though they seldom draw blood. The prion's bite is so delicate as to be hardly perceptible even when one's probing fingers are acutely sensitive because of the cold.

The blue petrel patch below the molly colony soon became another of my special Bird Island haunts. When the weather was good and the tussock dry, no more pleasant place existed. With a steady stream of mollies close overhead, I probed petrel burrows until my hands and wrists could take no more. To this day, I remember the mixed joy and pain of the burrows as part of the best of my Bird Island experiences.

Not so pleasant was the thick tussock in rainy weather, because the wet grasses soak one to the skin. Nothing this side of unadulterated water is wetter than drippy tussock. Rain or not, the appeal of blue petrels was so great that when it was too difficult or dangerous to do anything else on those foggy, wet days, I headed straight for my patch. I did not attempt to keep dry because in the long run it is easier that way, and so, soaking wet, I probed petrel burrows to my heart's content.

The wet tussock was not too great an ordeal, since Lönnberg House with its snug, dry quarters was close by. This is another example of how the efficiency of field work can be extended if proper living accommodations are available. Dryness is the most important advantage, not only from the standpoint of changing clothes, but also for maintaining records and preserving specimens.

One puzzling aspect of my studies was my continued failure to find diving petrels in my blue petrel patch. Blue petrels and Antarctic prions, yes, but divers, very few. John Croxall often walked through my special tussock on his way to or from his little macaroni colony and, oddly enough, reported finding lots of divers but no blues—this although before long I had located several separate blue petrel colonies on the slope. Certainly the blues were not confined to one small area.

Some minutes after leaving my blue petrel patch one afternoon, I became completely lost in fog so thick that I could barely see even a few meters ahead of me at times. When I attempted to get through the pass into North Valley, I invariably found myself at the edge of cliffs.

Suddenly from out of the mist stepped Peter Prince who, sensing my predicament, suggested that we return to Lönnberg House together. Getting through the pass on foggy days was easy for Peter, for he didn't depend on prominent landmarks; micro-habitats guided his way.

Before we returned to camp, Peter took me to some exposed tussock-free ground and pointed out minute differences between marginal, good, and excellent nesting habitats of the South Georgia diving petrel. On Bird Island this species breeds well above sea level in the crumbly summits of the high interior. Its habitat is so different from the lower, tussocky breeding slopes of the Kerguelen diving petrel that it is easy to understand why the sibling species remain distinct; moreover, the two breed at different times. On Bird Island a pair of Kerguelen divers lays its single egg in early November; the South Georgia diver lays its also single-clutched egg not much before the first week in December. This situation reminds one of the asynchronous timing in egg laying of the two species of giant petrels.

The South Georgia diving petrel excavates its burrow in hard gravel; the finer the stones and pebbles, the better the quality of its habitat. Unlike the hidden burrow entrances of the Kerguelen species, those of the South Georgian species are open to the sky. On Bird Island, one can stand back and take in at a single glance entire slopes of fine gravel riddled with hundreds of their conspicuous burrow entrances. Over all the highlands, the burrows number in the thousands.

The burrow of the South Georgia diver often runs straight back without a sharp bend, though some descend abruptly. Since the structure is also crumbly throughout, it is extremely difficult to repair once probed. This being the case, I didn't have the audacity to probe many of their burrows. Such examinations as I did perform ended in disaster, because the pair invariably deserted the patched-up affair, even though their egg was present.

One burrow that caved in practically to the egg chamber exposed the bird on its single, unsoiled egg. The bird scrambled out immediately and fluttered off. A skua immediately snatched it in midair and then descended to the edge of a sea cliff with its prey in bill.

The skua was doing only what skuas have been doing for eons. Just the same, I became so enraged that I dashed up and forced a release. The

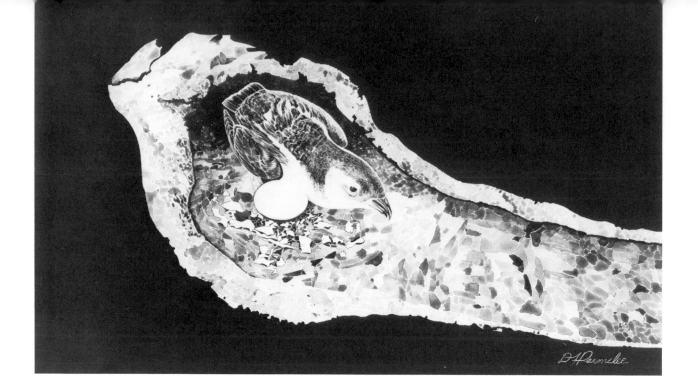

South Georgia diving petrel beside its egg in exposed burrow. Produced from a watercolor painting.

little diver intuitively plunged over the edge of the cliff with not one but two skuas in pursuit. But this time the diver held the advantage. I like to believe that it escaped to the sanctuary of the South Georgian sea.

For some time I carefully examined the nest chamber of the little diver I nearly fed to the skuas. The unstained, immaculate white egg rested on several whitish stone fragments not seen elsewhere in the tunnel, suggesting that the odd-colored stones had been deposited there by the birds. I doubt that they really had done this, but I nevertheless included these stones to the last detail in producing a watercolor painting of the bird in its egg chamber. I had no chance of sketching or photographing the diver in its chamber before it flew off, but such a sight is not easily forgotten. It is from the mental image of the bird beside its egg that I reconstructed the scene for the painting that had its beginning high in North Valley.

The blue petrels probably also breed in North Valley, though I failed to confirm my suspicions before leaving Bird Island. I had found a few burrows that I should have investigated because of the presence of detached feathers that belonged to blues. Whether these birds actually utilized the burrows for nesting or simply were investigating them is a moot question. All were in hard, stony ground and examining them would have required excavation with a shovel, but I was remiss in not having made the effort.

Many days slipped by before I made another attempt to reach Pearson Point. When I finally arrived there for the first time, on 7 December, my objective was to census the skua population. Many petrel burrows were on the peninsula, and judging by the numbers of blue carcasses near some of the skua nests, the total population of blue petrels must have been large. These facts had been known to Peter Prince for some time, unfortunately not soon enough to be included in George Watson's important 1975 publication "Birds of the Antarctic and Sub-Antarctic," which does not mention the species breeding on Bird Island, or even its probable breeding on South Georgia. Watson did believe that the blues probably bred somewhere in the South Sea area, though the only confirmed breeding areas known to him at the time were far away on Prince Edward, Marion, Crozet, and Kerguelen islands in the Indian Ocean.

Among George Watson's many responsibilities is the supervising of the bird collections at the National Museum of Natural History in Washington, D.C. He asked me to obtain, if at all possible, a skeleton of the blue petrel, since the museum's extensive Antarctic collection lacked one. So, one day when I found the nearly intact remains of a blue, evidently killed by a skua a short time before, I decided that it would do for a skeleton. The entire bird was frozen at Lönnberg House and eventually it reached California via a British ship, going to Palmer Station, and an American icebreaker. When it arrived at my University of Minnesota office a short time later, a former student of mine, Robert Zink, prepared a perfect blue petrel skeleton for the National Museum with the help of a colony of dermestid beetles—drab-colored insects whose tiny flesh-eating larvae are used by biologists in preparing skeletal material.

A place I visited often was Gony Ridge—a peninsula of tussock and cliff similar to Pearson Point and just east of it. And like the latter it had in addition to blue petrels nearly all the Bird Island species, including a small but superb colony of blue-eyed shags, numbering about twenty pairs.

No blue petrels to my knowledge resided in burrows beneath the shags, but many prions and Kerguelen diving petrels did. One diver in particular had a shallow burrow in what appeared to be pure guano. Every time I visited the shag colony I had to check it out, hoping all the while that its soiled egg would hatch before I left the island. On the morning of my departure, I stuck my finger in the burrow, felt the little diver give it the customary nip, then touched the familiar egg. If I had a single disappointment on Bird Island, it was my failure to see a diving petrel chick.

Despite the bad luck with the divers, my good fortune with the blue petrels continued. I had chanced on one of their larger colonies at the edge of a little swale on the east side of Gony Ridge, where petrel burrows honeycomb the pedestals of exceptionally luxuriant tussock. Naturally, I spent some time probing their burrows and soon came up with the ultimate prize of the season—a blue petrel chick. Holding that bit of bluish-gray fluff in my hand was a wonder. The long down that clothes the chick's small body gives the youngster the illusion of being much larger. Its nearly naked neck and head are so withdrawn in daylight that they are quite invisible. The living chick outside the burrow is simply an amorphic ball of fluff. No doubt I tampered a bit with reality in illustrating the head of the chick, though I suppose its head and bill must be extended during feeding in the burrow. Despite this somewhat unusual problem, I am pleased with the painting. There must be very few of its kind.

43

CHAPTER 6

Rapidly descending wandering albatross. Photographed 5 December 1976.

THE MONARCHS
OF BIRD ISLAND

Peter Prince glanced pensively toward Wanderer Ridge, turned to me, and said that Bird Island still belongs to the wandering albatrosses — even though the fur seals have taken all of the beaches and most of the tussock. From where we stood by the windows of Lönnberg House, the huge birds appeared to be a scattering of white dots on a background of green and yellow hills. As the weeks passed, I learned to appreciate more each day Peter's odd pronouncement.

At certain times of the year, nearly eighty thousand fur seals populate the little island. Not many of them reside along its northern coast, where towering cliffs dropping precipitously to the sea provide few beaches. Most are dispersed along the deeply indented southern shores whose rocky and sandy inlets provide ideal breeding grounds. Back from these beaches, low cliffs form a barrier to the interior, except at a few points where small streams break through to the sea.

It is up these rocky stream beds that so many seals make their way to the top of these cliffs crowned with tussock grass. From these levels, they are able to climb much higher, even a half kilometer or more from the sea. Despite the seals' clumsy movements on level ground, they are surprisingly agile in negotiating steep tussock slopes where human beings find the going rough.

This massive build-up of the seal population and consequent invasion of the tussock have been erosive and destructive. As I mentioned earlier, entire hillsides have been denuded, worn smooth by the grading movements of the seal hordes moving up and down the slopes. The seals have penetrated so many tussock areas that not many undisturbed ones are left outside the high interior. The "furries," as Peter Prince calls them, definitely have invaded the traditional courting and nesting grounds of the wanderers. But the wanderers yield nothing—not a single parcel of ground. In the face of seemingly impossible odds, they surrender no breeding spots.

In contrast to the huge throng of seals, not to mention the myriads of penguins, petrels, and other birds, only 1,400 to 1,800 wanderers breed

Portrait of male wandering albatross. Drops exuding from vicinity of the eyes are an erroneous illusion of weeping.

each year on Bird Island. Nevertheless, the wanderers control the scene—much like the California redwoods dominate every plant or animal within view. Bird Island belongs to the wandering albatross.

What makes the wanderer so special, indeed, one of a dozen truly outstanding birds of the world? Its great wings, for one thing. A large wanderer boasts a wing span of 3.35 meters (11 feet), longer than that of any extant bird except the royal albatross (*Diomedea epomophora*), a sibling species, that breeds in another region. The wanderer's long, narrow wing is perfectly molded to a long life at sea. Gliderlike, the wandering albatross soars effortlessly over endless waves on flights that circumnavigate the globe.

Wanderers require only a brisk wind. One finds them commonly in the latitudes of the roaring forties and howling fifties of the Southern Ocean. The doldrums along the equator create so effective a barrier that the wanderers seldom if ever cross to the Northern Hemisphere. Nor do they often penetrate the enormous pack ice ecosystem that encircles Antarctica to the south. On such a rare occasion in the pack ice, I saw one deep within the Weddell Sea close to the Antarctic continent at Cape Norvegia. The weather at sea that day was so calm that the old bird flapped more than it soared in a struggle to stay aloft. On Bird Island, the birds are conspicuously grounded on a calm day. When the wind blows hard there, which is most of the time, they are up and soaring.

In a good wind, the wanderer's takeoff from land is effortless. Its landing is quite the opposite—always clumsy and unpredictable. If a descending wanderer is aware of a human being in its path, it gives one no clue: The bird keeps on coming until one has to make a quick decision—move or risk decapitation. It is a nerve-racking moment on Bird Island whenever one of the big flying machines glides in unnoticed, sometimes a mere hand's-breadth overhead. The thought of being beheaded is bad enough; the awful roar of the wind rushing past the remiges of a rapidly descending wanderer all but gives one heart failure.

The landing itself is nothing short of miraculous. Often the birds crash down hard on open turf; nearly as often, they plow into the tussocks close by. They do well to manage a landing within a few meters of the nest or mate. However the landing, they seem content once they pick themselves up and adjust their feathers.

Some adults shy away from approaching humans. Before the more familiar seals and other birds they stand firm and clack their huge bills in the faces of their adversaries—as though the mere sight of the massive bill is not deterrent enough. On the nesting grounds, the strange ensemble of fur seals, giant petrels, skuas, and other birds somehow forms an acceptable mosaic of activity, despite the frolicking and commotion that often takes place.

Wandering albatross chick defying a young fur seal. Photographed 11 December 1976.

Human beings and their cunning ways pose a different problem. A person can, if careful, reach under an incubating wanderer and steal its egg. The old bird remains sitting as if nothing happened. Former whalers and sealers bent on obtaining fresh eggs for food decimated South Georgia's colonies of wanderers. A single egging expedition in 1923 probably destroyed half of the species' productivity on the island that year, when it took 2,000 eggs. According to Nigel Bonner, the large numbers of wanderers that formerly bred at Elsehul across the sound from Bird Island never did stage a comeback.

A plump, young wanderer is a table delicacy, I have been told; no doubt more than a few graced the Christmas fare of the whalers and sealers. Today the young scientists of Bird Island capture the birds for a different reason. By placing metal rings or bands with imprinted numbers and return addresses on the legs of these birds, they obtain vital information on their breeding behavior, schedules, life span, and, if the birds are recovered at distant points, their migrations.

How is it possible that man can catch and band with his bare hands a live wanderer that is quite capable of fending off something so formidable as a bull fur seal? All a person has to do is walk up to a wanderer, which doesn't give much if any ground, and grab it by its bill. If done swiftly and firmly, the great bird is quite helpless and hardly struggles. Once this is accomplished, the bander skillfully thrusts the forward end of the bird backwards between his legs while at the same time releasing the bill. This important maneuver results in one literally sitting backwards on the bird's body. Its head and awesome bill point harmlessly away from one's rear and its legs are free to handle. After attaching the band, the final step is simple enough — leap high and far!

Man and bird are none the worse for the operation. The wanderer may appear a little indignant, but if it truly is, it doesn't hold a grudge and usually remains on or close to its favorite ground. Sometimes my friends attach color bands on the legs of these birds for convenient field identification of certain individuals; or they put a temporary dye on the feathers so that individuals can be recognized easily from afar. Red or pinkish wanderers flying far from land may startle unsuspecting observers, but to the scientist they provide important data and demonstrate how incredibly far these birds range from their traditional nesting grounds.

By the time I arrived on Bird Island, most of the young wanderers had been banded by my companions. Since I was determined to cover as much of the rugged little island as possible during my short visit, I made a point of looking for any unbanded youngster they might have missed. Considering the many hidden and out of the way places where these birds could have been, I was impressed with how few young wanderers had been overlooked — I saw only four of 866 young that had survived until banding age.

Unlike the mollies that nest on the sides and tops of high, often steep inclines, even cliffs, the great wanderers claim broader, more level nesting areas, whether near the beaches or in high country well above sea level. Tussock-free areas composed of firm turf near the nests function as landing strips for the giants and dancing grounds for courting individuals. Often close to the firm strips are one or more small to fairly large pits, filled knee-deep with a sticky, evil-smelling goo. How these muck pits form I have no idea, but definitely they should be avoided.

According to Peter, one Bird Island visitor before my time had become so engrossed while photographing the mating act of a pair of wanderers that he inadvertently backed into one of the muck pits. His predicament elicited howls of laughter from his companions near by. Somehow he managed to retain his composure and his balance, snapping pictures despite all. I understand perfectly how he felt. Witnessing the mating of wandering albatrosses can command one's exclusive attention. The act gets underway on top of the pair's huge nest, no less, when the male plants his enormous feet in the center of his mate's back — which instantly sags pitifully under his weight. All the while, his massive bill tugs playfully at her nape feathers, and a little billing follows. There is much shuffling and adjustment of feet and feathers. By the time the all-important genetic contact is consummated, the female, pressed flat, appears done in. Still,

Male wandering albatross catches his adversary raping his mate. Photographed 3 December 1976.

both sexes show genuine affection and the bond appears strong. Anthropomorphically, one could make much of it.

Only once did I witness what appeared to be copulation off the nest. That particular mating high up on Wanderer Ridge was excessively wild, classifiable as a rape, it seemed to me. That it was exactly, for out of nowhere, thundering right past me, came the true mate. He flung himself headlong into the struggling pair. The enraged spouse then chased his competitor down the tussock slopes nearly to the sea, his great bill clacking as he went.

When I saw mating wanderers for the first time I instinctively grabbed my camera, only to run out of film after two or three frames. In dashing off to my pack for more film, I suddenly found myself thigh deep in the middle of a muck pit so sticky that I had all I could manage to get out with Wellingtons intact.

It's a mystery how I remained upright. Lucky for me no companions were close by to whoop it up; it was only the night before that Prince told his story of the poor chap stuck in the wanderer's pit.

Plodding back to Lönnberg House with tussock muck squishing in my boots and slowly working up my legs was bad enough. Cleaning up was worse. I finally discarded my trousers, socks, and underwear as a lost cause. The Wellingtons I baked over our coal stove, mentally thanking the Fids once again for such a marvelous luxury, but never once informing them of my accident. Eventually I got the boots fairly clean by scraping out the baked muck with a blunt knife. Afterwards I avoided albatross pits.

Wanderers are immune to the hazards of the pit; their big flat feet keep them on top. Sometimes, though, they step into narrow, partially concealed, streamcut troughs from which they cannot escape. One day

49

while we were crossing a meadow below Molly Hill, Peter said that he wanted to check a trough near one of the nesting grounds. No wanderers were in the nearly two meter-deep trench that time, but he had on a number of occasions extricated one from that death trap.

Wandering albatrosses are late nesters. As Nigel Bonner had said, eggs show up at Christmas time. A few pairs lay a bit earlier. The first wanderer's egg I saw anywhere was on Albatross Islet in the Bay of Isles, South Georgia, December 15 in 1974. On Bird Island the first any of us saw in 1976 was on December 10. On that day I was attracted to a setting female that snapped at a giant petrel waddling by her nest. She snapped at me, too, when I slipped my hand beneath her belly and felt the huge egg that weighs as much as 487 grams, or a little more than a pound.

The same day, high on the southwest slope of the mountain Tonk, I chanced on a broody female with an extraordinary egg, evidently just laid, for the creamy white shell had solid red dots scattered unevenly over its surface. The egg looked as though someone had touched it in a number of places with the tip of a brush dipped in bright red paint. The red pigment, whatever it was, did not rub off. I had never before seen an egg marked quite like that one, nor have I since.

Several days later, while walking along the slopes of Tonk, I recognized the brooding bird and decided to have another look at the special egg. I was astonished to find an ordinary, rather plain-looking one. So unexpected was this discovery that at first I thought I had the wrong nest. But I soon decided otherwise and confirmed my suspicions in noting a number of fine reddish circles; these were all that remained of the solid, bold dots, which apparently had burst, leaving behind only the faintest rings. The rings per se were not unfamiliar; I had seen them before, but was quite unable to explain their origin.

Despite all the albatross and petrel eggs that have been collected and deposited in museums around the world, modern-day authors perpetuate an error by early writers who described the eggs of the many birds of this order as being unmarked and dull white. Some members of this order do indeed have unmarked eggs; others, especially the albatrosses and some of the storm petrels, have boldly marked eggs, many handsomely wreathed.

Peter Prince made effective use of the breeding grounds of Tonk. When Peter conducted his study of the blue petrel, he hiked many times overland between Lönnberg House and Pearson Point. His study demanded so much time that sometimes he camped overnight among the petrels before returning to Lönnberg House. Having travelled to the west end of the island a number of times myself, and learning all about the tough stretches of tussock along the way, I understand why he established a food cache midway on the trail high on the slopes of Tonk. There he rested, ate, and sipped from a can of good Scottish ale.

Peter had a problem with this ale: It chilled during the cool days and cold nights. The British, as I learned, prefer their ale warm. It happened that close to his cache was a wanderer's nest still occupied by a hen that somehow had lost her egg earlier in the season. So, when Peter slipped his can of ale beneath her belly she readily accepted and tucked it away in her great incubation patch. She brooded that tin can faithfully as if it were her own egg. Each day before lunch, Peter took from the cache a cold can of ale and substituted it for the pleasantly warm one. Evidently the symbiotic arrangement went on for some time.

The complete breeding cycle of a single pair of birds may be defined roughly as the period from first arrival of the birds on their breeding ground to the fledging and departure of their young. The cycle for a pair of wanderers is extraordinary in being thirteen months long—far longer than that of most birds, whose cycles we measure in weeks, or a few months at best.

So protracted is the wanderer's cycle that females normally lay their single egg only once every other year. Since eggs are laid each year on Bird Island, it logically follows that two different groups of wanderers occupy the breeding grounds. The first group lays one year, the second group the next year, and the first group again the year following.

The dual arrangement is not so clear-cut as I have indicated; pairs that lose their egg or small chick early in the cycle are known to lay again the following year. On Bird Island, as much as 20 percent of one group returns the following year to repeat laying. Some mixing of the two groups is thus apparent. What happens in the event of an aborted breeding season for an entire group is a good question.

According to my British colleagues, such an aborted season occurred some years ago with Bird Island's gray-headed albatrosses—another species whose pairs normally lay a single egg every other year, despite a relatively short breeding cycle compared with the wanderer's. This suggests that other factors besides a protracted breeding cycle are responsible for the biennial egg-laying phenomenon.

In being aware of the biennial behavior of gray-heads, my friends were able to interpret better the results of earlier population studies that appeared abnormal for the species. One thing is certain; these complex problems would remain unresolved if banding and color-coding techniques were not available to the field biologist. The marked individual bird of known age and parentage is invaluable. The point cannot be emphasized enough.

For long periods each year, the two groups of wanderers occupy the

Bird Island breeding grounds at the same time, from about early November
to early February. To appreciate this remarkable overlap, we can refer to
Tickell's 1968 monograph on the species and concentrate on details of the
cycle, beginning in November with the arrival of adults in breeding condition. In the beginning males far outnumber females, but with increasing
female arrivals, courtship performances intensify with each passing day.
The female's grayer plumage readily distinguishes her from the male, especially when the two are side by side near their nest.

Egg-laying, from about mid-December to early January, is followed
by an incredibly long seventy-eight-day incubation period; hatching takes
place during early to mid-March. The chicks squatting at their nest sites
have to endure the cold austral winter when both parents forage at sea for
extended periods.

The chick is fed an average of three times every ten days, but is
known to fast for as many as twenty-four days. Likely the harsh winter of
Bird Island is partly responsible for its also extraordinarily long fledging
period of 278 days—in view of a fledging period of only 236 days for its
close relative, the royal albatross, which evidently does better in a more
hospitable winter environment. Feeding of Bird Island chicks continues at
the original breeding spots until fledging time, which begins for the strong-
est individuals in mid-December. Fledging extends into January. Both
chicks and their parents usually depart by February, at a time when members of the alternate group are hard at incubating.

Gray-headed Albatross

Light-mantled Sooty Albatross

South Georgia Pintail

Downy chicks of
South Georgia Pintail (top),
Blue Petrel (middle) and
Brown Skua (bottom)

The most exciting time to visit a wanderer's breeding ground is late
December when the two groups are simultaneously engaged in their respective breeding activities—at a time when courtship by members of one group
is still evident; some of them are either repairing old nests or sitting on
fresh eggs; feedings of last season's chicks by members of the alternate
group are still taking place; and fledging approaches a peak period. The
fledging of a baby wanderer merits comment.

The young wanderer, having been grounded for nearly a year, struggles
to break the tough bond between itself and the home turf. Day after day
one sees individuals stretch their untried pinions skyward, and leap valiant-
ly into the wind, only to be pulled down by gravity time and again. Prac-
tice is essential. The ubiquitous practicings are one of Bird Island's eminent
attractions.

Not all young wanderers make it to the sea. Every so often Peter
singled out a retarded youngster and said here was one that surely would
not survive to fledging. Some of these sorry individuals likely resulted from
late nestings, or perhaps from inadequate feedings by parents who have
the unenviable role of attending the giant youngster for so long a time.
For these unfortunate babies one quickly develops compassion, futile as
it is.

But for those chicks that lift off on their first great flight, there lies
before them the grandest of oceans, one that stretches unbroken around
the earth, one that abounds in squid and harbors few enemies. This maiden

*One of Bird Island's eminent
attractions—a young wandering albatross prepares for its
maiden flight and a long life
at sea. Willis Islands appear
in the background. Photo-
graphed 21 November 1976.*

53

flight propels the monarch bird onto the ocean that alone supports it for the next fifty or more years. How often the juvenile returns to land is anyone's guess, because at least seven and as many as twelve years pass before it attains breeding maturity. Conceivably it spends all this time roaming the seas.

Oddly enough, the wanderer's maiden flight has rarely been seen by human beings, even those scientists working daily among the birds. Aborted flights, yes, but not the one that finally takes the youngster out to sea. According to Peter Prince, regular and systematic counts had been made of young wanderers about to fledge in North Valley and elsewhere on Bird Island. Although these young showed a steady decline in numbers on the breeding grounds throughout the fledging period, the birds somehow managed to slip away unseen. He had seen the maiden flight only a few times during five field seasons. So, when Peter and Bruce burst into Lönnberg House on the cold and snowy evening of December 5, we knew instantly that they had encountered something special.

Sure enough they had—not one but two separate maiden flights at Johnson Cove. Of the many lengthy discussions that followed, one statement by Peter remains deeply imprinted, that the youngsters had walked a considerable distance to find just the right launching pad before taking off. I can't imagine a more graphic description of a fledging.

December 9 was another cold and blustery day on Bird Island. Freezing squalls kept blowing in from the south at regular intervals and blanketed the tussock slopes with soft, fleecelike snows that melted unevenly in places. Conditions in general were so miserable outside Lönnberg House that my companions found various things to do inside. Peter sifted through his molly data collected the day before while Bruce worked away at a painting. I was not quite sure what John was up to, but being cook of the day, I had the best excuse of all for being indoors.

Almost always we skipped lunch or at most took with us to the field a thermos of coffee and a little chocolate. Today was different. All of us were campside. What else to do but serve up a lunch? So, I gathered the leftovers and simmered some soup, which though labeled chicken clearly tasted like celery. If my lunch did little else, it spurred us to take to the hills. Despite the intimidating weather, we scattered far and wide. I clambered up through the wet tussock of North Valley and, in bursts of snow, checked my marked skua nests, though I could not find every one.

The skuas were downright vicious that day. From out of the snow clouds they screamed and dive-bombed relentlessly. Some struck resounding blows on my head and back. One hit the ax handle I was carrying so hard that it knocked itself silly. Battered half out of my mind by wind

Portrait of a wandering albatross chick.

and skua, I gave up the search and retreated down North Valley to a cozy spot away from the nagging discomforts, and finally found peace and a sky free of snow. Only then could I see the big wanderers up and sailing on a glider's wind.

One female in particular, a strikingly pretty hen with more gray in the plumage than is usually seen, kept circling in low above her much paler mate standing stolidly by the nest. For all of twenty minutes I snapped her picture each time she swept by, and also watched as she spun out over Bird Sound before returning again for another swoop.

It was during one of those return flights that I became aware of the upward spiralling of two young wanderers. Simultaneously, but not close together, they rose unsurely but steadily on juvenile wings that carried them forward on the most critical flight of their species.

Many meters above ground a blast of wind caught and turned the birds around, then carried them northward past a bold dome of grayish rock known to all on Bird Island as Bandersnatch. Northward the young-

55

sters went, now over the towering sea cliffs, now high above the sea. Now they were gone.

Had I really watched the magic flight so rarely seen by human eyes? Many times since, I have wondered whether that great desire coupled with a twist of imagination produced false images; among field biologists this is a common sensation. But no, I definitely had seen the maiden flight—two widely separated juveniles being carried over Wanderer's Ridge and past Bandersnatch shrouded that day by snow and ice crystals. This seemed the apex of a life filled with ornithological thrills.

Back at Lönnberg House, the quiet that followed my announcement of not one but two simultaneous maiden flights was something to behold. Not that my companions were unhappy with my good fortune. It was beginner's luck, something that everyone knows exists but cannot define, at least scientifically.

Peter, fatigued from climbing and draped loosely over his swivel chair, as I had seen him so many times before, suddenly jumped up and ran to the window. "There goes another young wanderer!" he shouted.

There it was, indeed, gliding southward high above Wanderer Valley toward Bird Sound. It was ferried on a shifting, waning wind and making the flight of its life. Three maiden flights in one day—must be a record of sorts, I mused.

No day passes without some excitement at Lönnberg House. This particular day that started on a low key had ended well. A celebration was called for. Being chef of the day, I prepared spaghetti with a good but frightfully hot, peppery sauce. Then I threw every skill I had into the baking of my first apple pie, starting with a tender crust and using more of the dwindling supply of fresh apples than I should have. Everyone seemed to enjoy dinner, though my culinary skills were enhanced, I am sure, by the cocktails provided earlier by my friends.

Nigel Bonner was correct when he implied that peak laying among Bird Island wanderers falls fairly close to Christmas, or shortly thereafter. Certainly it is much later than the other species of albatrosses nesting close by. Knowing that I would be leaving the island in late December, I entertained little hope in seeing a wanderer's chick. Considering its long incubation period, one would have to be on the breeding grounds in March, which lies on the dreg end of the breeding season for most southern species.

Fortunately for me, chicks of the gray-headed albatrosses begin to hatch shortly before Christmas. Having been informed that my departure date would be December 22, I spent most of the twenty-first roaming the

big rookeries of Molly Ridge on the sage advice of Peter Prince. That day, in the midst of snow squalls, I looked at hundreds of nests, but all but one had eggs or were empty. The one exception proved priceless—a fluffy downy. How carefully I handled that albatross chick—the first I had ever seen!

On one of its grayish legs I found a tick already deeply imbedded, on its head two more crawling about. Amazing. Somehow, I had never associated ticks with far southern, ocean-roving birds like albatrosses. Back at Lönnberg House, I was informed that ticks had been reported earlier from Bird Island, but Peter and the others had not seen any. The ones I found have since been identified as belonging to the genus *Ixodes*; those that parasitize gray-headed albatrosses are called *Ixodes uriae* by some authors. I had chanced on nothing new—only the joy of experiencing one's small discovery.

Little did I suspect that within a few hours of finding the molly chick, a helicopter would drop in unexpectedly and take me from Bird Island a day earlier than scheduled. During those hectic last moments, I quickly preserved the ticks in formalin (I was later informed that alcohol is the preferred preservative). I also made a quick pencil sketch of the chick's leg and webbed toes (for a future painting) and took with me from Bird Island that last day another precious albatross memory.

Gray-headed albatross chick approximately two days old. Found by author at Molly Ridge near Johnson Cove. Produced life-sized from a watercolor.

57

Running the Lönnberg House stream gantlet: young elephant seal followed by fur seals. Photographed 3 December 1976.

SATURDAY NIGHT AT LÖNNBERG HOUSE

Peter Prince said with authority that during the week things get pretty messy at Lönnberg House and, with that, he stooped to pick up the loose gear scattered about the hut. Looking up from an odd assortment of boxes and crates, he continued: Everything would be out of control if not for the Saturday cleanup! So, after the usual breakfast of canned tomatoes that smothered the sausage and our dwindling supply of hen's eggs, we rolled up our sleeves. This once-a-week necessity was anything but drudgery; we considered it a pleasant occasion topped by an evening of fun.

The first order of the day was to clear the deck of all furniture, paraphernalia, and trash. This had to be done to insure proper mopping of the floor, which had many hidden surfaces. Chairs, boots, and everything imaginable that was not nailed down were piled on the work benches. The big table between the bunks at the far end of the hut presented a problem. Being heavy and cumbersome, it could not be moved past the big coal stove called a Rayburn cooker.

Our dilemma was quickly resolved. We simply joined forces and somehow managed to lift and secure two legs and one side of the table on Peter's upper bunk. There it hung precariously while Bruce mopped feverishly below. All the while Peter was giving us explicit directions and a stern warning not to touch "the little lady." Somehow we got the table back in place without disturbing her.

Peter's little lady—a paper brunette in the nude—was tacked to the ceiling above his bunk. Looking down on Bruce's upper bunk was an equally captivating blonde. John and I in the lower bunks had none above us but enjoyed the many pinups that adorned the walls of Lönnberg House. Nightly discussions rarely got on the subject of women. We talked about the love life of seals and albatrosses, not people; our conversations were field oriented, nearly always related to our current studies. But the pinups filled a void in that unnatural, womanless world of ours.

SATURDAY NIGHT AT LÖNNBERG HOUSE

A visual clue goes a long way. It reminds a lonely man of that which he holds dear. This is the only explanation I can offer why my companions refused to eat from a bowl heaped with apples, placed conveniently on a shelf near the table. Little by little the apples spoiled, one contaminating its neighbor until all were decidedly unpalatable. The putrifying bowl survived many a Saturday cleanup. Perhaps the prolonged vision of a delicious fruit is worth many times its rapid consumption.

Saturday at Lönnberg House was not merely cleanup time. Peter was much too imaginative. He involved everyone in special projects. My first Saturday was spent helping to paint the hut's dingy ceiling a white enamel. A glossy surface would reflect much needed light on the work benches. Since light was such a valuable commodity, I volunteered to wash the hut's thirteen windows. Soon I had the panes sparkling inside and out. I was immensely pleased with the results, though my companions seemed overly enthusiastic. They didn't have the heart to tell me that my achievements would be short-lived: Within a day, all thirteen panes were spattered and whitewashed. The engulfing wildlife insured permanently stained windows.

Our most ambitious project was the laying of sheet linoleum. The rolls were big and heavy; moreover, they had to be cut and fitted around bunk legs, clothes closets, stove, and benches that were anchored securely to the floor. We avoided shifting anything that required a major upheaval. Despite good intentions we got off to a poor start. We made a bad mistake in attempting to unroll cold linoleum, which had been outside for days, protected only by a tarp. Quite a bit of it cracked before we had unrolled very much. Finally we hoisted the rolls up on the Rayburn cooker one at a time and let them thaw. Once again the old stove proved its worth.

Somehow we managed to get the linoleum down and laid. Had it not been for the mental and muscular prowess of Bruce Pearson, almost certainly we would have had a first-class mess. My admiration for Bruce's abilities grew daily, but particularly on that day of the Saturday cleanup.

For several days we tiptoed back and forth across the pretty blue and white linoleum, not once daring to enter the hut with grubby shoes. Although we dedicated ourselves unselfishly to the floor's preservation, for some reason the seams or cracks between the pieces of lineoleum began to widen, and the edges curled back in places. Finally came that dramatic moment when Peter Prince exclaimed, "To hell with it!" and clunked across the length of the hut in his cleated Wellingtons. Only then did Lönnberg House settle back to normalcy.

Not all Saturday projects took place inside. There were the wooden walkways over the streams and muddy flats to repair. Seals were always

Lönnberg House with its guardian fur seals. Photographed 20 December 1976.

smashing into them. The three sheds housing the food stores and genera-tor usually needed a little attention. And a huge green tarp draped over a stack of supplies required constant adjustment, since the gentoo penguins loved to scramble up the canvas and slide down its slippery surface.

Another favorite gentoo place was the open incinerator. What great attraction it held, other than a few warm ashes, is difficult to imagine. Whatever their motives, the gentoos badgered one another for a central spot in the structure. Several of them could be seen at the incinerator al-most any time standing upright ankle deep in ashes, their usually spiffy white fronts sooted head to foot.

Both fur seals and penguins loved to sit on the station coal pile that consisted of bags of coal stacked high, forming a sort of promontory over-looking our hut's front lawn. One old furry was so possessive of the pile that it became difficult for us to secure our coal. We found it not only ex-pedient but tactical to sneak in behind and snitch a bag before he realized what was going on. Once he caught me filching coal and chased me all the way to the porch. These were grouchy but harmless old bulls; when even-tually they abandoned the coal pile, others quickly took their place.

As if this activity were not enough, Peter Prince dammed the stream behind the hut to create a little pond, where various birds splashed vigor-ously. Seal pups converged at the pool for playful daily romps through the water, much like children cavorting in swimming holes.

No wild creature took in our outside activities with greater interest than the Lönnberg House skuas, George and Mavis. The birds had accompanied me all around the hut that first time I washed the windows, and stood together with heads tilted at the foot of my ladder, each following my progress up and down the rungs. Whenever I rubbed the glass, they methodically turned their heads to keep pace with my hand movements.

Not once did they grab the sponge or cloth when these items slipped from my grasp and fell to the ground, for they sensed what was edible and what was not. But let me step outside momentarily to dry a bird skin in the wind, and instantly they were ready to pounce. One could all but feel their attention and anticipation mount.

Bruce had similar experiences. While he painted the sides of Lönnberg House outdoors, both George and Mavis, of course, took in the activity. And, predictably, their eyes traced each stroke of his paint brush. But at one point Bruce climbed down the ladder, placed his paint bucket on the ground, and climbed back up with the brush in hand. This last bit of action proved too much for Mavis: She grasped the metal handle of the bucket and flew off with the works, spilling not a drop of paint. Animal behavior is predictable, but not always.

As soon as the Saturday chores and special projects were completed, we took to the hills. The chores were much reduced during those crucial times when our individual projects demanded our unstinted attention. One Saturday cleaning was skipped altogether. Field biologists understand this deployment perfectly. When one studies the breeding biology of a bird or seal, one conforms to the schedule of that bird or seal. A newly arrived chick or pup isn't the least concerned with station clocks. Yet, the business of scheduling studies afield remains one of the knottiest problems confronting the field biologist in that station or ship-bound individuals often do not think in terms of nonhuman activities.

Examples are varied and numerous. One humorous situation that comes to mind took place aboard one of our ships far at sea. Some of us were befuddled by the ship's schedule, which neither conformed to Greenwich time nor to that of our geographical longitude. Certainly it did not fit the field programs of our scientists aboard. The truth eventually surfaced. Ship's time simply suited the officers and crew members for making overseas phone patches to family and friends back home. What could be more logical?

Field biologists make out best among themselves. That great feeling of being freed of conventional shackles is why I so thoroughly enjoyed Lönnberg House; this, despite the necessity of giving much of our time to cooking and other chores of a nature that would have been provided aboard ship or at a large, land-based station. But even at Lönnberg House my

SATURDAY NIGHT AT LÖNNBERG HOUSE

British colleagues—among the hardest-working fieldmen anywhere—make an exception. They set aside one night a week, preferably Saturday night, to relax and raise a little hell. The one on K.P. that day makes every effort to come up with a fine dinner—Bird Island cuisine of the week.

Special dinners were not that easy to prepare. Our food stores though excellent were limited. The lamb in the deep freeze was kept for celebrations and holidays, and some of the camp staples, such as chicken eggs, were running low. My British colleagues rectified this situation by substituting penguin eggs. You will, no doubt, react instantly to my brash statement by asking, how is it possible for modern field parties to live off the land while preaching wildlife conservation?

Some years ago Matthews (1929), in writing on the birds of South Georgia, and after having seen literally tens of thousands of incubating macaroni penguins, described the species' clutch size as being one egg. In a sense he was right, for a pair of macaronies normally incubates one egg and raises a single chick. What Matthews did not realize is that the pair actually lays two eggs; the first small and soon discarded, the second large and incubated until hatched. One rarely sees both eggs in the nest at the same time. I satisfied my own curiosity on the subject by carefully marking several small eggs and later returning to the nests, which then held only large, unmarked eggs.

My British friends took only the small eggs before their being discarded. But how, pray tell, could I top a meal of penguin eggs? Still, I felt duty-bound to outdo everyone at least once—and I did just that by salvaging the macaroni penguin carcasses from the two birds my Bird Island collecting permit allowed.

Pair of macaroni penguins with their single viable egg. Photographed 18 December 1976.

SATURDAY NIGHT AT LÖNNBERG HOUSE

I had never before eaten, let alone cooked, penguin. Many explorers long before our time had survived on them. Fortunately for me there was at Lönnberg House a cookbook written by a Fid knowledgeable in the ways of survival. To the last detail I followed his copious directions on how to prepare penguin.

Evidently it was important that I wrap the two penguin carcasses in porous gauze and, out of reach of skuas, let the wind batter and knock them about for most of a week. On the morning of the special night I took them down, diced each into stew-sized chunks and boiled them with salt for eight hours. The intensely dark meat that I poked with a fork every half hour appeared delightfully tender and juicy. How could my friends top this?

Next I made some of my popular spaghetti sauce, added a liberal portion of hot peppers and proudly served up the penguin. All of us plunged in. The first chunks went down far better than I had hoped. Not before they hit the hold of our stomachs did we experience a strange transformation. Up from our bellies came the most awful bubbling and sickening sensation any of us had ever known.

I looked first at Peter. His was a sullen face, indeed. It stared impassively at the plate before him. By then John had turned a shade of green, and Bruce had the startled look of someone who couldn't believe his senses. Even then my courteous hosts said nothing. But when I threw down my fork in disgust, they howled and quickly followed suit. We all agreed that in our combined experience nothing in all this world compared with macaroni penguin. If we lost our dinner of the week, we gained a lively conversation piece, not only for the rest of the evening but for many a day following.

A statement in the Fid's cookbook seemed appropriate. Referring to the preparation and cooking of penguin, it advises that if all else fails, the only recourse is to take the penguin and "fling it as far as you possibly can." So, I took my penguin stew to the open window and flung it to the winds. Old George immediately cleared the ground of all competitors, then helped himself to a big chunk. But he didn't bolt it down: He held it for a long minute, then tossed it.

I never did see skua or anything else eat my penguin stew. Little by little it disappeared. Possibly some greedy giant petrels or sheathbills flew off with the chunks, only to deposit them uneaten in the hills. Even the bony carcasses went begging—a rare occasion to be sure.

Now that my British friends have long survived the penguin feast, they will be amused to learn that my great fiasco has a logical conclusion. In collecting the pair of penguins I chose not to shoot them for fear of disturbing the breeding birds at the big rookery. I knew that one doesn't easily kill a penguin simply by whacking it on the head. The resilient little birds, like punching bags, are immune to blows. So, I gave each a good whiff of ether from a supply given to me earlier by Peter. Had I recalled my basic chemistry, I would have realized that ether is highly soluble in fat; the chemical quickly spreads throughout fatty tissues, rendering the flesh unfit to eat. Blowing in the wind and boiling on a hot Rayburn cooker has no redeeming qualities.

On those special Saturday evenings, after a good meal and providing that the weather was fair, the Fids engaged in a unique form of recreation: They sat quietly at the beach where the stream that flowed past Lönnberg House entered the sea. Up and down this stream, seals traveled to and from areas inland. No other avenue close by afforded a safe trip for man or seal—so dense were the defended territorial harems everywhere else along the beaches.

Fur seal pup. Photographed by the author during his first landing on Bird Island on 2 December 1974.

An incoming elephant or fur seal invariably poked its head out of the frothy inlet to survey the stream cautiously before running the gantlet. When finally it made up its mind to move inland, it pulled all stops. It dashed headlong up the stream bed, throwing up great clouds of water along its path. Those harem bulls residing along the stream reached out occasionally to give the running seal a nip.

By and large the stream was safe ground—sort of a no man's land. A seal charging up or down stream passed my colleagues within half an arm's length, literally, paying not the slightest attention to man or beast. About the time it reached Lönnberg House it slowed down considerably, as though to contemplate the next move. My friends insisted that I partake in this activity, if only once before departing Bird Island. Frankly, I had had my fill of seals—I needed no additional encounters. But the more I resisted the more adamant they were that I give it a try.

I finally agreed, reluctantly, though I knew all along that it must be safe. Fids of all people take care of their guests. On one of these rare golden evenings—a "dingal" evening as Bruce would say—my friends set me down on gravelly beach and shell beside the little stream, then abandoned me.

On each side of me were swaying hulks of seals, big bulls squabbling over cows, and babies, endless numbers of them, scrambling all over the place. Among hundreds of seals were penguins, skuas, giant petrels, and flocks of sheathbills. The latter quickly singled me out, though thank goodness the big harem bulls nearby paid not the slightest attention. Their fierce odors so close were something never to be forgotten. True, I had for several weeks fought my way through throngs of seals; sitting defenselessly among the beasts was quite another matter. If my heart ever skipped a

65

few beats, it did so when the first furry broke water and charged up the stream in one gigantic explosion of spray and pebbles.

It was a huge one, and it seemed to come straight for me. By the rules of the game, the beast should have charged right on by, looking neither right nor left, but instead it came to a screeching halt beside me. The wetted fur standing on its nape was no less erect than my own. Even now I vividly see its slowly turning head, its big bloodshot eye rolling sideways, its bristly whiskers barely not touching mine. I sat transfixed. The end of a very good life at hand.

With a mighty snort that drenched my face, he turned and bolted up the stream. How long I sat there, a blob of putty, I can't say, but for the next hour or so I remember furry after furry charging past me, though none like the first had stopped to look me over.

Because of my harrowing experience, I really expected a little consolation back at the hut, but received not one bit. Peter Prince assured me that on many similar occasions a big furry actually had rubbed its whiskers against his cheek. Rubbing whiskers with a fur seal, imagine! Oh well, I had survived the hazing and now was a true fellow of the Lönnberg House fraternity. Still, Peter warned me once again that conditions at the stream were different from that of being charged by a potentially lethal territorial bull. He got no argument.

On other occasions I found myself going back to the beach to sit among the seals simply for the fun of it. With me, however, went a special stout club for the close encounters. As predictable as these seals are on the stream bed, one cannot afford to lose sight of the exception. After all, hadn't old Mavis flown off with the paint bucket?

The Lönnberg House fraternity found it a challenge to photograph the seals running the stream-bed gantlet. For Bruce it must have been really exciting catching all that motion and splashing water on movie film. For me, equipped with only a still camera, it was no less rewarding, especially the time I captured three seals—two furries and an elephant—all galloping up the stream bed at once.

The Fids have still another form of recreation. This one has more subtleties than first meets the eye. It is a Saturday night attraction—a game called Ukkers. Above all else, it confers respect in the social order of Lönnberg House.

British Ukkers reminds me of several boyhood contests. It is a party game of sorts, consisting merely of a pair of dice, round buttonlike disks of several colors, and a single squarish playing board. This last has a well-marked but hazardous trail on which the disks are finger-pushed from one delineated spot to another. The idea is to move the disks around the board from a starting point to a finish line as fast as one possibly can on the toss of dice.

If one's disk lands on an opponent's disk of a different color anywhere along the trail, the captured disk is sent back all the way. The fun of the game is to pick off your competitor's disks, especially when close to the finish line. Pure and simple, Ukkers is a game of chance, but my British friends insist that beneath the simple facade of dice tossing lies a contest of mental skill. The longer I played the more convinced I was that they really believe this.

Winning at Ukkers was not the point of the game, despite the pomp and ceremony that accompanied each contest. Once the serious game got underway, I was amused by the sudden change in speech and mannerisms of my genial and polished companions. The usual courtesies gave way to rudeness and cynicism. Peter, confronting John head-on, blistered him with a finely executed snide remark relating to some recent encounter or incident. John quickly retorted with something equally devastating. Between the sparring and jabbing, Bruce managed to get his pokes in.

As the game wore on, the tempo of derisory remarks increased. No doubt the rounds of Scotch malt that we reserved mostly for the Saturday night occasion incited the players to greater verbal attacks. Only Rod Stewart's "Atlantic Crossing" maintained a steady drone in the background.

Things never got so bad that fists flew. Although the hurts and frustrations of the past week all poured out during Ukkers, one would really have to look hard for any hidden, deep-seated animosities. There simply wasn't time for major incidents to develop from little ones; pent-up emotions were nipped in the bud. When the top winner finally emerged from Ukkers during the early hours of Sunday, all was forgiven and soon forgotten. The victor basked momentarily in glory while the vanquished tripped off to bed.

At first I was spared the ribbings and jibes, but not for long. Peter especially loved to zero in on American idiosyncrasies, taking me to task on everything ranging from sports to politics. He was convinced that our cities were violent and dangerous; New York City held such a fascination for him that my sheltered, academic life-style disappointed him. But Peter was the first one to defend me on issues big and small. It was good that I became enmeshed in the Ukkers squabbles. How else, other than caressing seal whiskers, could one be acceptable to the Fids?

Sunday was just another work day on Bird Island. Admittedly there were times following an excessive bout of Ukkers that things got off to a late start, but our studies and mental attitudes surely benefited by those Lönnberg House Saturday night specials.

CHAPTER 8

Teal Pond. Photographed 29 November 1976.

SCAVENGING TUSSOCK DUCKS

Among the many unusual Bird Island species is a small teal-sized duck that looks like a duck but does not behave much like one. Its feeding habits are peculiar. So far as I could determine, these Bird Island ducks feed extensively on animal remains, and this could be an important adaptation, considering the extensive winter snow cover. During winter the nonmigratory ducks are thought to forage along the edge of Bird Island's open sea which rarely freezes over.

Although sometimes referred to as teal, these strange ducks are best called pintails, the currently accepted name being yellow-billed pintail (*Anas georgica*). The race or subspecies endemic to South Georgia and Bird Island is the South Georgia pintail (*A. georgica georgica*), a close relative of the somewhat larger and paler brown pintail (*A. georgica spinicauda*) of South America and the Falkland Islands.

Except for the yellowish bill, bright in breeding males and a good field characteristic for separating the sexes, the birds have a rather somber body plumage. The speculum, though not really eye-catching in males, hardly exists in females. The neck of both sexes is long and sleek and thus is similar to that of other pintails. Hardly a flashy duck, the South Georgia pintail certainly does not lack character.

Two to five of these pintails can be found most any time just outside Lönnberg House whenever the hut is occupied. They favor the area where an open-ended drain leading from the kitchen spills dishwater over the ground. Every time water is discharged down the drain the pintails gather to sift the fine food scraps.

Soapy water does not deter them in the least, and one concludes that few items, however small or soapy, escape them. Extremely quick and agile afoot, they run circles around the skuas that also occupy the area, though the latter quickly monopolize any large food items. When the skuas abandon a scrap of food, such as a bone too large to swallow, the pintails are standing by to pick the leavings.

SCAVENGING TUSSOCK DUCKS

A windfall in food occurs whenever a seal dies, which happens often during the breeding season around Lönnberg House. The first birds at a seal carcass are the northern giant petrels. With their powerful bills, they quickly pluck out the eyes; then they go after the entrails. A greedy flock of a half dozen giant petrels can strip a seal carcass to its hide and bones in a few days. But before that happens, other species claim their share of the carcass.

The tough skuas, though considerably smaller than the giant petrels, wade in among the latter and take what they want. Not all feedings are gruesome affairs. They can be comical. Once, our Lönnberg House skuas struggled with a long section of seal intestine that was still attached by one of its ends to the carcass. When George flew off with the loose end of the gut, he was abruptly jerked backwards, head over tail.

For the much smaller sheathbills, approaching the carcass is not so simple. They stealthily dash in and tear at a fleshy hole previously opened by the skuas or giant petrels. Sheathbills are shifty birds and forever flitting about near their food, as though the feeding had to be consummated in bits and dabs with split-second timing. This behavior enables them to dart in and snip flesh from the open wound of a living fur seal that has been bitten by another in the battle for mates. The sheathbills often enlarge the wound until healing seems improbable.

One might surmise that the delicate little pintails wait their turn to pick at the bones and small scraps left by the larger predators. Wrong assumption! As soon as there is a small opening in the seal carcass the ducks dive headlong into the hole, which conceals from view their bills and at times even their heads.

The head is methodically withdrawn time and again for surveillance, but it is not unusual to see both giant petrels and pintails simultaneously picking at the same carcass. The ducks are so clever in maneuvering that not many are caught unaware. Unlike the giant petrels that acquire grisly scarlet heads while gorging on the bloody flesh, the fastidious pintails remain remarkably clean by dipping frequently into streams or pools of water.

Many times I watched the Lönnberg House pintails screen the waters of several streams that flowed near the hut. Occasionally I saw and even photographed them feeding on filaments of green algae, and no doubt they were finding minute animal life, but other than algae, I found nothing that looked edible in those waters. Certainly, I was not about to collect our station pets to examine their stomach contents! Probably, the pintails fed in the tussock ponds, where one could find several of them almost any

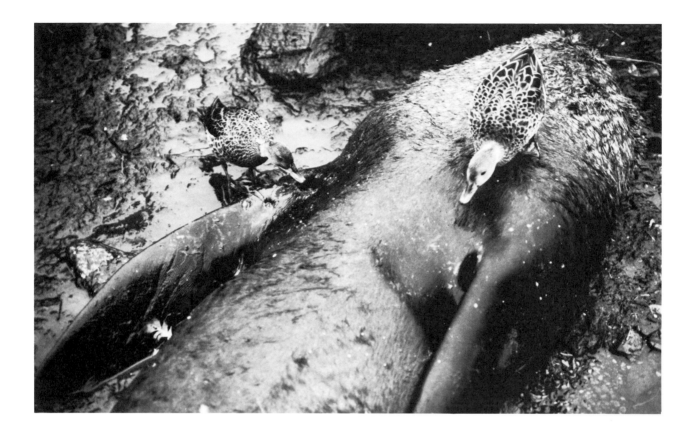

time. And very likely, the birds fed at the seashore, but the beaches when occupied by breeding seals were off limits. I once observed feeding pintails in the rocky inlets of Cooper Bay during my first trip to the east coast of South Georgia, though at the time I had no idea what they were eating.

A few references mention their feedings on the coastal shores of Bird Island, but the most extensive research for both inland and coastal feeding behaviors and foods on the pintails was conducted in Cumberland East Bay by Milton W. Weller—a University of Minnesota colleague and neighbor of mine. Weller (1975) stated that the ducks usually fed in ponds and at the seashore with head and neck underwater or by upending; diving in the fashion of dabbling ducks was a regular activity in deeper ponds where fairy shrimp were abundant.

He made the point that the pintails fed "occasionally" in the soggy soil of poorly drained areas, at the edge of pools or melting patches of snow, or along streams. In addition to fairy shrimp, the foods taken by the pintails included amphipods, snails, small clams, diptera, nematodes,

South Georgia pintails feeding on a seal carcass. Photographed 27 November 1976.

71

filamentous green algae, and sea lettuce of the genus *Ulva*, although plant foods were thought to be of minor importance during the breeding season.

Most remarkable was that throughout Weller's informative report no mention was made of the bird's insatiable appetite for meat. True, expansive Cumberland East Bay with its respectable elephant seal population holds few fur seals, whereas tiny Bird Island at times is inundated with thousands of fur seals, and the carcasses of their dead are everywhere.

My guess is that the pintails of South Georgia and Bird Island feed on a variety of foods, including carcasses when they can get them. Bird Island pintails have adapted to an extraordinary supply of carcasses made available through the great breeding colonies of birds and mammals.

One cannot help but speculate about the behavior of pintails at Cumberland East Bay during the heyday of whaling and butchering at Grytviken. But the ultimate question is: What foods maintain the non-migratory pintails of South Georgia and Bird Island during the long austral winter, when ice covers the ponds and streams, and snow the land to the edge of the sea? Weller believes that marine filamentous algae may supplement the diet after the breeding season. I would include any small invertebrates available to them in winter. Certainly the Bird Island pintails would pounce on the first available carcass.

Our Lönnberg House pintails appeared to be exceptionally tame. I suppose this was partly because they were accustomed to us, but they did dodge and avoid us as they did the seals and skuas. Sidestepping was a way of life in their crowded living quarters. Invariably the ducks registered alarm when approached directly by man or beast, and sleeping individuals slept with an open eye.

By and large the pintails were harmonious, unobtrusive creatures. The only antagonism observed between two birds of the same or different sex took place at the kitchen drain pipe, where a hierarchy of sorts was established over feeding rights. A dominant male or female suddenly bristled and charged its adversary of either sex, driving it from the food source. However, there were no real struggles—only inoffensive bluffs.

At various inland ponds the pintails, usually flocked, were also docile. Certain birds appeared mated, but birds of the flock were so complacent I would have sworn they were not breeding. John Croxall would not have agreed with me, for he said that some pintails had eggs as early as 14 November. He had accidentally come across a nest in his travels near Cobbler's Mound, a short walk east of Lönnberg House. I am sure that he did not then fully appreciate how difficult it is to find a South Georgia pintail's nest—especially if one sets out to find one. Peter admitted that not many nests were found on Bird Island, though he certainly was familiar with them.

My British colleagues' apparent lack of interest in these fantastic little ducks was at first difficult for me to understand. But, of course, they had the likes of albatrosses to take up their energies.

Milton Weller's party had failed to find a single pintail nest during an entire season afield. This is understandable, because the birds in Cumberland East Bay are dispersed thinly and not nearly so concentrated as they are on Bird Island. What Weller did find was a brood of three ducklings of the speckled teal (*Anas flavirostris*)—a new breeding species for South Georgia.

I searched long and hard for this species on Bird Island, but found none. At the same time, I was confident that I would find easily a dozen nests of the pintail, not only because of their great abundance, but also because of what appeared to be prime habitat. Wide stretches of tussock grew luxuriantly to the edge of their ponds. But all this profuse, seemingly ideal nesting habitat yielded not one nest; although I crisscrossed and crossed again numerous tussock banks and slopes, actually avoiding the easily negotiable open areas. Many times I told myself that the ducks simply were not on eggs, though I knew better. On occasion I saw individual males, even within the pond flocks—clue enough that a mate was off incubating.

Ducks or no ducks, the skuas were the main attraction, and I devoted most of my time to them. While looking for skuas in North Valley high above Lönnberg House, I found one of their nests that was particularly difficult to reach on the cliff side of a bluff. It was on a spot of moss attached precariously to the rock. The dive-bombing skuas coming off the top of the bluff didn't help matters as I inched along the front, hanging on with both hands for additional support.

Since this skua's nest had only one egg, I returned frequently to time the laying of the expected second egg. On one such trip at dusk, I caught the faint flash of a pintail whirring out from the skua's bluff, but a search of the few sparse patches of tussock in the vicinity produced no nest. On returning to the site early the next morning, 23 November, I flushed a pintail from eggs nestled in a shallow platform of down and stems not far from the skua's nest. All four eggs were well concealed in a patch of tussock grass tucked away in a pocket of the rock wall. It was truly a cliff nest, and a pretty one at that. Never had I experienced so great a thrill in finding a duck's nest.

I marked the four eggs, since they appeared fresh and probably repre-

73

Male South Georgia pintail. Produced from a watercolor.

sented an incomplete clutch. Here was an opportunity to determine the unknown incubation period, but on subsequent trips I discovered that the pintail had deserted. This surprised me, since the bird on leaving the nest had made a beeline for Lönnberg House—far below the bluff—and I had the feeling that the bird was one of our pets. I could not be certain of this, however, because none of the Lönnberg House pintails had identifying bands or markers.

Later examination of the four eggs showed that they were not fresh but that all had tiny embryos. So the clutch of four, which would be small for most northern ducks, was complete. Still, I was perplexed by the color of the eggs; I had expected to find cream-colored or pale olive-green eggs, as previously described for the species, but found four eggs of a color I had not seen in the eggs of any of the North American waterfowl. The color does match closely those egg colors of the ashy-headed goose (*Chloephaga poliocephala*) I saw on occasion in southern Argentina. According to a chromatic scheme of colors illustrated in Robert Ridgway's "Color Standards and Color Nomenclature," United States National Museum, Washington, DC, 1912, the color of the preserved shell is pale pinkish buff; that of the living egg probably comes closest to being pale cinnamon pink.

In two additional clutches I saw that year, the colors were essentially pale cinnamon pink. One of these, a clutch of five, Peter and Bruce found on 5 December beyond Macaroni Point, in a dense, tussocky area known as Bottom Meadow. The nest was on a gentle slope near the top of a ridge, some distance from a large pond where pintails congregated; it was concealed and situated well above ground in the tussock. The duck flushed when Peter and Bruce accidentally walked close to the site. Since its nest was only a few steps from a conspicuous incubating giant petrel, I had no difficulty finding it some days later on 13 December. The duck was not on the nest at the time. As I stood waist deep in tussock grass examining the eggs, a pair of pintails circled in close, whistled shrilly, and flew on.

I don't know whether the birds were actually the pair of this nest, but subsequently we found only cold, deserted eggs. At Peter's request, I brought one back to Lönnberg House to hatch it artificially above the stove. But it was placed too close to the fire one evening and the embryo died, if indeed it had been alive when it was taken from the nest.

The last pintail nest I saw was on a steep side of Molly Hill where the tussock is so profuse it is almost impenetrable. When the duck flew out, I decided to leave no tussock grass unturned and soon came upon the nest with its three pinkish eggs. Much like the other nests, this one also was well concealed above ground, essentially a platform of dry stems and bits

75

of tussock grass mixed with dark down, the color of which resembles Ridgway's "Chaetura drab," although each individual feather had a pale grayish, nearly white center or nucleus. Out of fear of losing this nest to desertion, I bypassed the site on future trips to Molly Hill, except for the last one when accompanied by Peter Prince on 21 December. The three warm eggs were surely viable, though we failed to see the duck.

On numerous occasions I flushed single pintails from steep tussock slopes, and no doubt some of them had nests. But unless the duck flushed directly from eggs, the odds of finding the nest were poor. Now that I know how few nesting records exist for the species, I wish I had taken more time to search. Whether nesting or not, the Bird Island pintails are so much at home in the tussock that it is a pity they were not named "tussock duck."

At Lönnberg House one day I made the offhand remark that I was puzzled by not having seen a brood of ducklings at any of the island's many pintail ponds. Peter said that was not surprising at all, then explained that the ducklings live in the tussocks and are virtually impossible to catch. He further said that only one duckling survives, at least only one is usually seen with the duck.

I thought this last statement of his outlandish, although by this time I was convinced that Peter Prince was a remarkable person, capable of remarkable observations and deeds. As I presently scan my personal field notes, I find reference only to single Bird Island ducklings, and not many at that. I never did see a brood of five, four, even three or two. In the beginning, I thought they would be commonplace.

Exceptions are the rule in a biologist's world. It was Peter who later reported a brood of three attended by three hens in an isolated little pond high up in a meadow. I told him in jest that what he really saw was not a single brood of chicks but three broods with one chick apiece—each with a hen attending a social gathering! The enigma deepened when John, who had just returned from the same meadow, said two of the three hens had flown off, leaving one with a brood of *five* ducklings!

Obviously the family life of these pintails warrants further study. What role the male parent plays during incubation and fledging periods is a vexing question. On the surface it appears that he has much more of a role in these family affairs than most North American drakes familiar to me, but on this point I am only guessing.

One fact of which I am certain is that on the ground even the recently hatched Bird Island pintail is greased lightning—like rats in a tunnel, as Peter described them, referring to the tussock corridors that form a bewildering maze of passageways and provide an easy escape route for the ducks. Still, I wanted to catch a duckling, to photograph and sketch it. My chances of doing this, according to Peter, were practically nil.

Peter had a special surprise for us on 8 December. When we finally discovered what it was—a Sub-Antarctic form of fur seal (*Arctocephalus tropicalis tropicalis*) seen only on rare occasions at Bird Island—a plan already had been set for all of us to go out and photograph it and record its vocalizations at close range.

It was an opportunity too good to pass up. The seal was resting on low rocks washed constantly by the surf. Even though these rocks were a short walk down the coast, we had to decide how best to approach them, considering the large number of the usual Antarctic fur seal (*A. t. gazella*) on the beaches.

Our final plan was not to attempt to follow the seashore but to cross over a low ridge of tussock worn smooth by seals and, from there, descend a fairly steep bank to the sea at a point not far from the special seal. For the last hundred meters we threaded our way along a wall of jagged rocks, until we found ourselves within a stone's throw of the magnificent creature.

By that time a flock of twenty curious sheathbills had alighted near us, and from then on our every move was watched with studied anticipation. Sheathbills sense or at least associate food with man and his disturbing influence on wildlife. But we gave the sheathbills nothing this day.

On the return trip across that stretch of denuded tussock, Peter and Bruce spotted a pintail and its single duckling. Without the protective tussock cover, the chick could not easily escape us. Peter finally cornered it in the blind end of an exposed corridor. The recently hatched pintail was a perfect model. I wanted to claim it then and there, but I had vowed earlier that I would disturb no wildlife in the vicinity of Lönnberg House. So I let it go, after a frustrating attempt to photograph the duckling in light so poor my light meter did not respond. With it went my hope of sketching a Bird Island duckling.

My hopes were rekindled a week later. High up near the pass in North Valley I nearly stepped on a hen pintail that fluttered and flopped before me on the mucky turf. When she leaped high into the air and came down again a short distance away, I knew she had a chick close by. Then I saw it—only one—and watched it run and disappear in a tussock corridor.

I don't know how long I chased that duckling. I do remember that in a state of jubilant desperation, I reached down through a thick canopy of tussock grass into the water of a half submerged corridor and came up with a struggling chick. As elated as I possibly could be, I also was ashamed of my predatory behavior. I felt somewhat like a skua with a human conscience.

Conscience or not, I tucked that chick in my pack and dashed straightway for Lönnberg House with one thought in mind. By the time I reached the porch the sunlight was right for photography, so I decided to postpone the sketching and photograph the bird.

Bad idea! No colleague was handy to hold the bird while I snapped its portrait. For the next five minutes I was reduced to photographic trickery of a kind I do not condone—that of attaching a string to the leg of a bird to prevent its running away. But I had no choice: I had the camera, the sunlight, and the subject. Without the string, I would have no subject. I swallowed my principles and set the stage.

No sooner had I lowered my camera when the chick struggled and peeped. From all directions came flying pintails, no less than seven, the most I had ever seen at one time on the mossy front lawn of Lönnberg House. They circled without relent, their whistlings and scuttlings something to behold. One hen ran to the chick right under my nose paying me no heed. Then from out of nowhere came old George, the Lönnberg House skua, and carried off the prize. Not to be outwitted by George, I somehow retrieved the duckling, but the chick was dead and I desolate.

The chick illustration, which I now value, was constructed much later from the specimen. I had preserved on film the colors of the chick's soft parts. A statement in my field notes that I later found useful was that the living Bird Island duckling has a conspicuous yellow spot before and above the eye.

Not high up on Wanderer Ridge, a pleasant walk from Lönnberg House, an intriguing complex of interconnecting shallow pools is appropriately named Teal Pond, because invariably one can find the Bird Island ducks on its murky waters. Coincidentally, twenty-nine pintails were present when I first visited the pond on 29 November. That day, the ducks flew off when first approached but then turned back and splashed down within a pebble's throw of where I sat quietly beside one of the pools.

The beauty and appeal of Teal Pond derives partly from its well-appointed setting. Its waters lie within lush bryophyte banks and tussock, and are circled by courting wandering albatrosses performing love rituals. Among the wanderers, defiant skuas and hustling pipits attend eggs or chicks, and not far away giant petrels of two species incubate complacently. Best of all, there are no seals—though some are not far off.

East of Teal Pond the ridge unexpectedly drops away to deep, scabrous, seal-inhabited ravines and almost abruptly rises again as Cobbler's

White-chinned petrel at burrow entrance. Photographed 17 December 1976.

Mound. The latter is riddled with little grottoes—the summer burrows of white-chinned petrels, the ones referred to earlier as the singing cobblers or shoemakers. Incredible numbers of these white-chinned petrel burrows occur not only at Cobbler's Mound but also at innumerable places on Bird Island; so abundant are they that the species must be one of the island's commonest birds. A few of their cavelike burrows are thin-roofed, running closely parallel to the surface of the ground. On occasion I stepped through the flimsy ceilings, which I immediately repaired with turf and tussock. One time I broke through so close to the egg chamber that my foot ended up beside the incubating bird.

Architecturally, the egg chamber itself has an outstanding design. The single, large white egg rests on a pad of tussock stems that in turn is supported by a raised platform encircled by a neat little trench, presumably scratched out by the bird's sharp claws. The miniature moat drains away soil seepage and keeps the platform and egg dry within the burrow, which can be quite wet. I have often seen flooded and consequently abandoned burrows of other kinds of petrels, but not one of this species.

Some burrows of white-chinned petrels extend a long way back from the entrance, much farther than one can usually reach. Even so, one should not probe their burrows without extra heavy gloves, for a bite by these birds is painful, as my good friend Nigel Bonner discovered the time he showed me my first burrows at Hound Bay, east of King Edward Cove. Poor Nigel's fingers were horribly lacerated by the old bird he tried to pull off the egg that day.

At Lönnberg House one evening, Peter Prince asked Bruce Pearson to open and partly expose a number of these burrows nearby at Cave Crag, where the white-chins commonly nested. Bruce carefully made an opening near the egg chamber of each and covered the artificial holes with concealing lids that he could remove conveniently for nest checks. How I wanted to see and sketch one of Bruce's newly hatched shoemakers before I departed Bird Island! Alas, all I saw were unhatched eggs.

Vertical cliffs form the lower sides of Cobbler's Mound all around, except for the one connection to the island. The mound's east side falls off to a deep gorge, partly ringed near the top by nesting light-mantled sooty albatrosses. From the bottom side of the gorge rises an orange-lichened pillar of rock that supported perhaps a half dozen nesting pairs of

79

Antarctic terns that season. Perched on the peak of the pillar was a single Dominican gull on its nest of moss. On rock prominences near the pinnacle resided several more pairs of nesting terns; below them, hordes of seals.

Whenever I was in the vicinity of the gorge I could not resist peeking furtively over the edge of the cliff for a look at this little ternery. However careful my movements, I invariably triggered an explosion of terns that rose rapidly in a clamorous protest. Instead of pounding me, as usually the case with these birds, they would vent their frustrations on the incubating gull. One after another the terns dive-bombed the gull which settled lower and lower until nearly flattened on its nest. The terns came frightfully close in their stoopings, but they appeared not to strike and certainly did not dislodge the old gull that occasionally snapped back.

I had visions of getting down to the colony for a closer look because of my research interests in gulls and terns. According to Peter, a rope ladder was the only safe means of getting down and up again. He then showed me a metal stake that had been driven into the turf near the top of the cliff by a former observer and used from time to time to secure the ladder. I did not press Peter for use of his ladder and, consequently, never did descend to the ternery. Just as well—it was the only known one for Bird Island and merited consideration. Gulls were even scarcer. I was aware of only two nesting pairs on the island.

All this exceptional scenery and wildlife at Cobbler's Mound enhanced my visits to Teal Pond, so much so that on the cold, crystal clear and wind-free morning of 6 December, following a rather heavy snow the night before, I dropped everything I had planned for the day and headed for the ponds with cameras and tripod. The quickest and safest way to the ponds was up the rocky stream beds, rather than over the hummocks. Many seals occupied both places, but I had learned that the majority of those along the streams were less aggressive.

The day was wonderful, the finest one could wish for. On the stony flats beyond Lönnberg House, where several streams joined and formed laceworks of running water, stood a coy little group of gentoo penguins, apparently immature birds that guarded several mock nests of stones. About a half dozen of them occupied the eggless nests this morning. They stood grandly resplendent in the early sunlight. I stopped a moment to photograph them.

I stopped once more, to photograph a bull fur seal on a flat-topped boulder that it had claimed for its very own. His frosty, coruscating mane shone so brilliantly that I took special pains in framing him against la Roché, Bird Island's highest peak.

SCAVENGING TUSSOCK DUCKS

Captivated by the sparkle of everything before me, the walk to Teal Pond that normally requires ten minutes took most of an hour this day. Water in the creek beds was frozen solid in many places; that still flowing leaped and splashed over icy rocks and bones of seals long dead. The tussocks that normally hold their heads high were bowing under the whitest of snows. The contrast between white and green was breathtaking.

Teal Pond was frozen over and a dozen pintails were strung out along its snowy edge. The ducks were skittish that day and took wing at first sight. They didn't go far. When circling back for a landing, some not too perceptive individuals hit the ice, skidded, and crashed harmlessly into the soft bank. Once again, I flushed the pintails but this time broke the ice along one side of a pool with my tripod. In short order they were back and quickly found the open water. There they swam or simply stood by the pool that mirrored each lovely contour. As I sat for most of an hour watching them, I hardly felt the cold. How lucky I was to be here—a stranger—among all these splendid creatures of a natural world uncluttered by human litter. At times like this, I am haunted by thoughts that our biological investigations will be for nothing if we cannot find ways to preserve segments of our wild kingdom. How would it greatly benefit man to know much about a species if we cannot prevent its premature extinction? Yet without man's concern and assistance, however token, premature extinction is a certainty for many life forms now threatened by our mechanized societies.

Cobbler's gorge usually lies in shadow, but today the first light streaming in low above the glimmering heights of South Georgia was deflected on the rim of its cliffs. A photographer's light at its best. So, I gathered camera gear, concluded my sentimental bout with Teal Pond, and headed for the gorge to photograph the light-mantled sooty albatrosses. On the way, a pair of dive-bombing skuas quickly brought things into perspective. Eventually I reached the gorge, which today had a broody sooty half asleep in the cold morning sun.

The old bird was so accommodating that I approached it within finger's length to observe closely its remarkable eye, certainly anything but a dull spot. Rather, it is a handsome grayish olive eye with an outstanding white feather line behind it. The unusually pretty gray of its neck and head plumage impressed me even more. I cannot decide which gray is the more elegant—that of the sooty or that of the gray-headed albatross.

Returning to Teal Pond, I found the pintails I had encountered earlier, but their friendly mood had vanished and with it the last chance for more photographs, for that day was my last among them.

CHAPTER 9

Northern giant petrel attending single chick. Photographed 11 December 1976.

STINKERS

The giant petrel is the sea bird that comes to mind whenever my thoughts wander to the Southern Ocean. Southern ships and giant petrels are natural partners, and I never fail to think of one without the other. For days on end in the windy latitudes, these are the birds a person will see circling or doggedly trailing behind a moving ship far at sea, and the ones that will be swimming in the still waters beside the ship at harbor town waterfronts.

I suppose that the giant petrel's passion for food is the main reason it clings to ships, awaiting the inevitable handout of scraps from the cook's galley. Its notorious eating habits have earned its widely used name "stinker," for when it comes to bad table manners, the giant petrel has no peers among sea birds. Not even the rapacious sheathbill is in its class.

After watching a flock of giant petrels feed, one might conclude that anything edible would do, and it is a fact that the birds eat most anything dead or alive that is animal. But even among giant petrels some order in food preferences exists, at least within its genus *Macronectes*.

As mentioned earlier, two species occupy Bird Island. The two look so much alike in size and plumage coloration that one often recognizes the southern species (*M. giganteus*) by its green-tipped bill, and the northern species (*M. halli*) by its brown-tipped bill. On Bird Island the two nest side by side, but an important difference exists between them with respect to breeding schedules, the northern species being much the earlier. Differences in feeding habits appear to be equally important, though not nearly so obvious. I slowly became aware of these differences near Lönnberg House, where giant petrels would battle one another for a share of a seal carcass. Without exception, all that I saw at the carcasses were northern giant petrels, even though several pairs of southern giant petrels nested as close by as Cave Crag.

My colleagues said that my observations were valid, but then confided that they had not spent much time on Bird Island studying the feeding habits of giant petrels. Presumably, the southern giant petrels of Bird

STINKERS

Island, inasmuch as they do not feed regularly on seal carcasses, fly off to sea where they find cephalopods, crustaceans, and fish.

Fish? One cannot assume too much regarding the feeding habits of giant petrels in general, because in checking the literature on the subject, I quickly found reference to the observation that in the Indian Ocean, near Isles Crozet, the northern species "regularly fishes" in coastal waters, whereas the southern species "rarely does." It would seem to be not so much a question of food preferences, for I am reasonably certain that regardless of species a giant petrel is not all that finicky, but that somehow, in those areas where their ranges overlap, the two manage to partition the food resources in a manner advantageous to both. The two tend not to dine together.

During the few afternoons I spent indoors at Lönnberg House, while sketching or attending to specimens given to me by Peter Prince, I had good opportunities to watch northern giant petrels swarm at fresh seal carcasses beside our porch.

Through the open front door of Lönnberg House, I watched upwards of a dozen of them strip a big carcass of its flesh within a three-day period. The flesh surely would have disappeared sooner had it not been for the antics of dominant individuals that strutted like old-world vultures before the feast. The bullies flipped their partly spread tails upward, leaned stiffly forward on outstretched wings arched sharply downwards, then boldly confronted their competitors. With heads bloodied red and dripping seal guts, they shuffled and maneuvered for the best places. During such interruptions, our little Lönnberg House pintails slipped in among them for their share of flesh.

The usually mute giant petrels are anything but that during their feastings and quarrelings. I can do no better than George Watson (1975), who describes their vocalizations as "nauseating retching noises, loud hissing, vicious bill snapping." The awful retching sounds rising from their bellies and the gory head drippings make the feeding spectacle seem revolting. Giant petrels are so adept at bad manners that one inevitably accepts the humorous side of their behavior. No question, they are the clowns of the southern seas.

If one only steps outside on the porch of Lönnberg House, the feasting flocks explode. Some of the stuffed birds barely lift off the ground after running headlong into the wind; others are so weighted down with carrion that the best they manage is a clumsy dash over the turf, their great flat feet producing loud scufflings as they go. No sooner does one go

84

Southern Giant Petrel

Northern Giant Petrel

Northern Giant Petrel feasting on carrion

Paired South Georgian Blue-eyed Shags

back inside though than these gluttons return to feast anew with un-diminished appetites.

Incubating giant petrels of both species are not so prone to run or fly off, though the mate standing nearby often does. As with the wandering albatross, one can walk up to an incubating giant petrel and snap its picture. One does so at some risk, however, for the birds have a nasty habit of squirting vomit directly at a person, as many a camera novice has discovered; and to be splattered with giant petrel vomit is something not to be taken lightly!

Many petrels eject a copious yellowish or orangy stomach oil when threatened or handled. Wilson storm petrels eject a clear oil so fine that it has marvelous penetrating qualities; the oil's odor, not terribly objectionable, is somewhat musty and hard to dispose of. But one is subjected to much more from giant petrels than mere stomach oil, especially from those having recently fed on putrid animal remains. Little wonder people call these birds "stinkers."

I soon learned the knack of forcing the birds to regurgitate by probing them gently with a pole from a safe distance. One old handsome bird—if you can honestly call any giant petrel handsome—I made retch several times before taking its picture. When finally only dry heaves resulted from

Incubating northern giant petrel (lower left) and southern giant petrel (right). South Georgia lies beyond Bird Sound with its single iceberg on 3 December 1976.

85

my probing technique, I stepped in close for a head portrait. Alas, my subject had a hidden reserve that showered me and my camera and put us both out of commission for some time.

Once in the air the giant petrel is no longer the ugly, clumsy bird seen on the ground. It is a magnificent flyer, and even though some claim that it lacks the grace of other flying petrels, it competes with the best of them for sureness and endurance. Often I have watched their circling and dipping flights from the fantail of a ship in rough seas, and never ceased to be amazed by the big bird's ability to extend its lowest wing tip to within a scant millimeter of a breaking wave. The soarings of these and other sea birds are broken only when galley refuse is dumped overboard.

Settling within the floating garbage, the giant petrels quickly assume their role as stinkers, hogging the food. Fortunately for the smaller Cape pigeons and storm petrels, the galley scraps quickly disperse over the moving waters and soon all partake in the spoils.

A strange sight indeed is a row of standing giant petrels on the slightly exposed surface of a dead whale or elephant seal afloat at sea. At a distance the birds appear to be standing on the surface of the water, which of course they cannot, despite their large webbed feet and swimming abilities. Immense flocks of the smaller petrels feed on the oil slicks that trail for hundreds of meters behind a floating carcass. This uncommon spectacle is exciting not only for the passengers aboard, but for seasoned crew members as well, judging by the numbers that come topside.

On windy Bird Island the giant petrels launch themselves from high perches to circle the land and sea, taking advantage of the cliff eddies with the same carefree abandon shown by the mollies and wanderers. A peculiar circling flight of the northern giant petrel that I watched consisted of repeated low sweeps over the land. Flying individuals suddenly would assume a stiffness suggestive of threatening displays at a seal carcass, holding their heads slightly upwards and uttering not unpleasant sounds. I had no idea what these birds were doing; much to my dismay, I was not too successful in capturing the special aerial flight with a camera, so have since taken up the challenge with simple half-tone sketches.

Both southern and northern giant petrels nest at various elevations over much of Bird Island. Earlier I mentioned that the two often nested in proximity, so close to one another in places that I easily captured both in the same photograph—giving the illusion that the two occupy identical habitats. If, however, one were to take the time and energy required to visit a number of breeding grounds where the ranges of the two overlap, one would reach a different conclusion—as have the ornithologists who

Portrait of chinstrap penguin.
Produced from a watercolor.

have studied the habitats. Southern giant petrels tend to nest in more exposed places than the northern giant petrel, for the latter evidently prefers
heavier vegetative cover.

The northern giant petrel's preference for heavy cover on Bird Island
is readily seen along Peter Prince's well-worn path leading to Johnson's
Cove. On both sides of the path, dense growths of tussock support impressive numbers of these birds. Several of them nested so close to the path
that I had to sidestep them to avoid being nipped or squirted.

Johnson's Cove was another of these special Bird Island areas that
held lots of birds, but since it also was one of my colleagues' principal
molly study areas, I preferred to work other sites, except for an occasional
visit. Among many attractions, the Cove had a large gentoo colony where,
at its seaward edge, nested seven pairs of chinstrap penguins. To my knowledge, these chinstraps were the only ones that bred on the island that year,
though Nigel Bonner later told me that several pairs bred, or least formerly,
near the beaches of Bird Sound in the vicinity of Natural Arch. Often
standing among the nesting gentoos and chinstraps at Johnson's Cove were
several king penguins.

The kings are the prettiest of the penguins, even more so than their
close relative the emperor penguin (*Aptenodytes forsteri*) of the high Antarctic. Had I not seen thousands of king penguins in their big rookeries on
South Georgia, I surely would have been tempted to wade among the gentoos and chinstraps at Johnson Cove for a closer look at the kings—which
do not nest at all on Bird Island, though they breed as close by as Elsehul,
a short distance across Bird Sound.

At Johnson's Cove the gentoo-chinstrap colony is situated in a low basin confined except at its beach side by spectacular tussock ridges and sheer cliffs. Elephant seals often sit among the nesting penguins for reasons not known to any of us. Since these seals are easily stampeded by humans, it is unthinkable to send these living bulldozers into a path of penguin eggs and chicks. The presence of several elephant seals among the gentoos and chinstraps convinced me not to enter the colony for a closer look at the king penguins. I had wanted to examine their heads closely, for during my first encounter with them in 1974, I had noticed a gorgeous green sheen to the otherwise blackish crown of the adults—a condition I had failed to see in any of the many photos taken of the birds. With this coloration in mind, I had a great desire to paint the portrait of a king penguin.

On Bird Island one is easily sidetracked by many wildlife activities going on at once, but no matter what the diversion, one doesn't go far before encountering the ubiquitous giant petrel. I had seen hundreds, if not thousands, of these birds on their nests in many places and never failed to examine the eye of each incubating bird. No two birds appeared to have exactly the same eye pattern, and in this respect they differed from one another more remarkably than they did in plumage coloration. The irises ranged from white to nearly black, from clear to highly freckled or speckled. Many appeared fish-eyed. To my knowledge, no one has been able to explain this extreme variation in eye color. At one time I was satisfied that at least the white-plumaged birds of the southern species invariably had dark irises—until I found one with pale-lemon-colored eyes within my principal study area at Palmer near the Antarctic Peninsula.

Many giant petrels breed at Palmer, but all are of the southern species. The only Palmer record we have of a northern giant petrel is of a single bird that followed a ship all the way from an Argentine port. At Palmer, with so much to be done with skuas, gulls, and terns, we didn't plan a special study of giant petrels. But, as in the case of Bird Island, one doesn't go anywhere in the Palmer study area without encountering these birds, and my students and I simply could not resist taking notes on them. We knew that they had long incubation periods, but not quite so long as the ones timed by our gull-man, William Fraser, who recorded a sixty-five-day mean incubation period for a dozen birds under observation. Conroy (1972) recorded a mean incubation period of about sixty-one days for thirty-seven eggs on Signy Island. This suggests that the harsher climate of Palmer may prolong the period by a few days—an assumption that will have to be verified.

By color banding adults at nests, we confirmed earlier observations that both sexes incubate the egg. Both also sit on the chick for about eighteen days, then simply sit beside it unless inclement weather develops. By the end of the second week of growth, the initial down is gradually replaced by another, heavier down that assists the chick in achieving self-regulation in temperature, or homeothermy, by the end of the third week. Then a strange turn of events takes place: Both parents fly off and leave the helpless chick unguarded in the nest for hours on end, returning to feed it from time to time.

Why these plump, conspicuous chicks are not instantly pounced on by the ever-present skuas and other predators is a vexing question to me and to David Murrish, a Palmer-based colleague, who studies the species' physiology. Perhaps the nest site, having been defended successfully for so long a time by the incubating parents, retains some protective qualities. But if these qualities really exist, they are invisible to us. We simply have no explanation. The chick's bite certainly is innocuous, and although the youngster squirts vomit at a surprisingly early age, it is hardly a match for a predatory skua or unrelated giant petrel. Yet the big predators ignore them!

William Fraser, who spent more than twelve months at Palmer, doesn't think it strange at all, for he once observed a six-week-old giant petrel successfully repel a brown skua with vomit. Bill's hypothesis, based mostly on one of his gulls that evidently had been squirted, is simply that the vomit easily penetrates the predator's plumage, causing the feathers to lose their insulating qualities by becoming limp and penetrable by water. Well, perhaps a six-week-old chick can generate and direct enough vomit to repel a tough skua, but a three-week-old one? All I can say is that not all has been said concerning giant petrels.

Whether on Bird Island, Signy Island, or at Palmer, the young giant petrel remains at the nest site for a long period—about 115 to 118 days

89

on the average. At Palmer the young fledge in winter from about 26 April to 19 May. Peak fledging occurs during the second week of May.

Unlike their fledglings that quickly abandon the breeding grounds and fly incredible distances, the parent giant petrels remain close to their Palmer nesting spots all year. Throughout the winter, the pairs return time and again to their eggless nests composed of old limpet shells and stones. At that time of year, the ice-encrusted nests often are covered over with snow unless exposed by the winds. Exposed or not, the old birds sit on or above their favored nests in the dead of winter.

According to my overwintering graduate students, the mock nestings produce no eggs. Giant petrel eggs do not appear in the Palmer nests before early November, when the austral spring is anything but clement. In the high southern latitudes, November is decidedly wintry despite the lengthening daylight. Early spring storms often inundate the incubating birds with fresh snow. On occasion I have seen only the tips of giant petrel bills protruding from the drifts. No harm befalls the eggs protected by the parent's brood patch, but such storms disrupt the early breeding schedules of the much smaller Antarctic terns incapable of breaking free of wind-hardened snow. The terns abandon the egg before becoming entombed and later overcome their losses by laying again under better circumstances.

Climatic conditions are less severe on Bird Island, where the nests of the two species of giant petrel are far less spartan. The Bird Island nests are chiefly tussock piled high, forming elevated mounds slightly bowled on top. The two species appear to have similar nests and both structures, superficially at least, resemble those somewhat larger nests of the wandering albatross.

Both giant petrels of Bird Island nest commonly among the nesting wanderers. I did not often see even minor fracases among the adults attending these many nests, but among the youngsters mysterious confrontations sometimes develop. High up in North Valley one day I came upon a baby wanderer that evidently had occupied and claimed for its own the eggless nest of an immature southern giant petrel. For whatever reason, these prebreeding giant petrels commonly sit on empty nests among incubating wanderers and giant petrels. According to Conroy (1972), prebreeders return to their natal colonies about their fifth year; males breed before females and about a two-year period elapses between the bird's first return to the colony and its first breeding.

We shall never know what prompted the young wanderer to occupy that particular giant petrel's nest. The displaced giant petrel appeared frustrated and, even in my presence, nudged the wanderer in a continuous but

Displaced southern giant petrel "prebreeder" from its eggless nest by a wandering albatross chick. Photographed high up in North Valley on 20 November 1976.

fruitless endeavor to push the larger bird off the nest. The wanderer chick paid it scant attention; occasionally it clapped its bill when somewhat annoyed with its smaller neighbor. Some days later I found the albatross chick on the same nest, with the giant petrel sitting on the bare ground nearby, a most unusual twosome.

Thanks to Conroy and others, much information has been compiled for the giant petrels. Most of what we know concerns the adults and, like so many other species, information is lacking on the lives and whereabouts of the subadults. It has long been known that giant petrel fledglings circumnavigate the southern oceans rather than fly northward like the skua and gull fledglings. It was no surprise to us that our Palmer-banded young giant petrels began turning up on opposite sides of the earth in New Zealand and Australia, thousands of kilometers from our study area. We were, however, surprised at the short time it took these youngsters to travel halfway around the world. Some made it within a three-month period. To date, a dozen of our young giant petrels have been recorded in the Australia-New Zealand area. Considering that only a few hundred young up to that time had been banded at Palmer, the recovery rate is exceptionally high for such long-distance flights.

An important factor in the high recovery rate is the existence of bird-banding clubs that constantly look for banded birds. These groups patrol coastal waters in small boats and are able to approach the big birds when the petrels struggle to lift off the waters on calm days. What sort of wind speed does a giant petrel require to lift off? According to colleague David Murrish, an adult male requires a wind velocity of 4.8 kilometers per hour.

Banding data can be perplexing. One seemingly old giant petrel we observed at Palmer carried a United States band that was not one of ours. We reported its number to our bird-banding center in Maryland and later were informed that although the bird had been banded previously at Palmer, it was reported as dying when last seen in the tropical waters near the Fiji Islands in the Pacific. Whatever its plight at Fiji, it surely recovered, for ten years later it was sitting on an egg in our Palmer study area.

91

CHAPTER 10

Shag Rocks. Produced from a watercolor.

BLUE-EYED SHAGS

Shags, also called cormorants, are strange looking creatures that are classified with pelicans and a few other families having similar characteristics. An important anatomical one shared by all members of this class is a peculiarity of the foot. All four toes of each foot are connected by webs—a unique condition in birds, referred to as totipalmate and made possible through a forward and inward rotation of the hind toe, which in most birds points backwards, in the opposite direction of the three front toes.

Shags have special characteristics that when taken together set them apart from other totipalmates. These include a long body and fairly long neck, short to moderately long wings, long stiff tail, short legs, and a slender bill with a pronounced hook at the tip. An unusual feature of the fully developed bill is the lack of external openings to the nostrils. Adults fly and perch with their mouths partly open because they breathe through their mouths.

Breeding shags of both sexes often develop plumes of the head, neck, and flanks. The name shag may have been derived from the shaggy appearance of these plumes, worn for a short time only each breeding season. Shags of all ages have featherless patches surrounding the eyes. Their also naked and wrinkled throat, or gullar sac, can be stretched to accommodate a fish.

Shags dive from the surface of the water and chase fish at various depths down to at least sixteen fathoms, but then return to the surface with their prey. Diving and underwater swimming are facilitated by their heavy bones, less pneumatic than those of most other totipalmate birds. According to E. P. Todd, Director of the Division of Polar Programs for the National Science Foundation, shags swim rapidly up to a fish and grab it from behind; while peering down through the clear waters off Massachusetts, he actually saw one catch a fish. These fish-eating birds also can change their specific gravity and can sink slowly under the surface of the water in the manner of loons, which they resemble in size and shape. In

BLUE-EYED SHAGS

the Northern Hemisphere, people often confuse the two. This particular problem does not occur south of the equator, where there are shags but no loons.

Approximately thirty species of shags are distributed broadly over inland and coastal areas of the world, excepting the north central regions of Canada and Siberia, and certain islands of the Pacific. Many inhabit marine coastal areas, but they are seldom seen at sea far from land. Their unexpected presence at sea was an indication to the seafaring explorers of old that land was close by. Following his discovery of South Georgia, Captain James Cook wrote that "shags and soundings were our best pilots."

Shags north of the equator are dark-bodied birds of similar heritage, considered by ornithologists to be a distinct assemblage. In the distant past a few of these northern-type shags penetrated southwards into Africa, Australia, and South America, where they exist today. Shags of a different ancient heritage evolved in the Southern Hemisphere. They are easily separated in the field from their northern cousins because they have conspicuous white underparts that contrast with dark upper parts. The blue-eyed shag is one of the white-breasted members of this southern group.

Blue-eyed shags do not have blue eyes: Their irides are distinctively brown. A cyanine blue ring of naked flesh that surrounds each eye is responsible for the name, which is much preferable to "blue-eyelidded shag," for the latter would be intolerable.

As if the blue eyelids were not enough, both sexes also develop bright yellow, or orange, fleshy excrescences at the base of the bill, called caruncles. Since enlargement of the plumes and caruncles occur at the time of courting, these structures are thought to be linked to breeding behavior, but their precise function is debatable. All agree that the adornments add a dimension of color and excitement to the already handsome bird.

Blue-eyed shags are circumpolar in the Southern Hemisphere. They are a complex group that has been subdivided into as many as five species, and as few as one, with seven subspecies. Debates continue as to the status of each species or subspecies, but none has been so heatedly discussed as those concerned with the birds that occupy South America. A widely accepted view proclaims two closely related but distinct species of blue-eyed shags, *Phalacrocorax atriceps*, the one often referred to as "blue-eyed shag," and *P. albiventer*, the one commonly called "king shag."

Anatomical differences between the two are slight. The so-called blue-eyed shag has much white on the side of the head, causing a high cheek line dividing the black and white plumage; during the breeding season it vividly shows a few white feathers on the upper back, called the dorsal patch or bar. The king shag has a low cheek line and no dorsal bar; it reputedly has more highly developed caruncles.

Recent studies indicate that the two types of shags coexist at numerous (but not all) breeding colonies on the continent, where mixed pairs and birds with intermediate plumage patterning have been identified. Some authors suggest that the South American blue-eyed shags are polymorphic, that is, they are a single species (conspecific) that exhibits two or more morphological patterns, such as high and low cheek lines. The problem is further complicated by the fact that the shags of the Falkland Islands constitute a highly homogeneous population of the king shag type, with no apparent polymorphism.

Clearly the shags of South Georgia and Bird Island are of the blue-eyed shag type, although they have highly developed caruncles somewhat like those of king shags. An undisputed characteristic of these birds is that they are measurably smaller than the South American, Falkland, and Antarctic Peninsula shags. Mainly because of their small size, they have been classified as a distinct subspecies, the South Georgian blue-eyed shag (*Phalacrocorax atriceps georgianus*). Museum specimens alone will not solve the knotty taxonomic problem of these shags. A better understanding will require a carefully planned and prolonged field study on mating and descendance at a mixed South American colony of blue-eyed and king shags.

South Georgian shag colonies range in size from a few to upwards of 30 pairs each. Bird Island has only three small colonies. Those on Pearson Point and Gony Ridge support only 15 to 20 pairs each, judging by the number of nests. The Cardno Point colony holds even fewer pairs. South American colonies of blue-eyed shag types very often consist of thousands that contribute to an important guano industry. Shag guano is nitrogen-rich excrement that splashes all around the nests at breeding sites. Thick accumulations of guano are mined profitably for fertilizer.

Nests at all three Bird Island colonies are embedded in sloping ledges of barren guano high on the sides of sea cliffs. They are easily reached from above by climbing down droopy tussock banks. Walking between the nests is tricky business, because on the brink of a cliff slippery guano can be treacherous.

Bird Island shag nests are substantial pillar-shaped structures of shredded tussock, seaweed, and guano, not quite as high as one's knee, and slightly bowled at the top to contain a clutch of two or three eggs. The eggs are thick-shelled, pale blue when fresh, and often have white chalky incrustations. The readily stained eggs turn brownish when incubated.

BLUE-EYED SHAGS

Both sexes incubate, and each sits unmovable on the eggs. On Bird Island one can step up to an incubating shag, look it squarely in the eye, then stroke its handsomely iridescent back—at some risk of being scratched by the sharp bill. One often observes both members of the pair are on the nest at the same time, one on the eggs, the other barely on the rim. Although no sexual dimorphism is apparent in blue-eyed shags, males measure slightly larger than females. The difference though slight is perceptible even in the field at close range when paired birds sit side by side. Paired shags with their swaying sinuous necks hooked lovingly together compose a very pretty picture.

Vocalizing birds give few clues as to their sexual identity. Shags are notoriously quiet most of the time, but nonetheless are capable of producing a variety of unpleasing gutteral noises, croaks, and grunts. These are given mostly at the breeding sites when paired birds vigorously rub, bow, and curtsy. They also vocalize to some extent when disturbed. Dislodged birds fly swiftly from the ledges out over the sea, only to return immediately to their nests. The noisy out and back flights are much more impressive than their muted vocalizations.

Several species of birds resided with the shags at the colonies. Gray-headed albatrosses incubated on similar pillar-shaped nests alongside the shags. Puncturing the guano beneath the nests of both were the burrows of white-chinned petrels, Antarctic prions, and Kerguelen diving petrels. American sheathbill eggs were in niches of rock outcroppings, surrounded by guano.

One of two sheathbill nests at the Gony Ridge colony was so exposed to the sun that I tried to photograph the pair at the nesting niche, but the skittish birds invariably dashed off long before I got close. Imagine my surprise, then, at finding one of them in such a stupor that I actually lifted her off the nest. I knew it was a she, because I felt the egg about to be dropped from her swollen oviduct. Gently putting her back on the nest, I waited expectantly as a midwife.

At the precise moment that egg was laid, my foot slipped on guano and I failed to observe which end of the egg emerged first. Years ago I was amazed to see the pointed end of a sandpiper's egg appear first, after having read somewhere that the blunt end of an egg is the first to emerge. This much I can say for a newly laid sheathbill egg still covered with sticky mucus: Its boldly patterned chocolate-brown spots and blotches can't be easily rubbed off.

The female's behavior following the laying seemed odd. She fell head-first off the nest and landed with her breast pressed flat on the ground,

Incubating blue-eyed shag at the Gony Ridge colony.
Produced from an ink drawing.

her tail and legs pointing stiffly upward. I thought she might be dying, but after three minutes she recovered; she stood up, returned to the nest, investigated its contents, then sat on the egg that proved to be her first of the season, if not her very first. Observing the laying of eggs is a useful field technique for determining the sex of certain birds, such as sheath-bills, that show little dimorphism.

For some unexplained reason the shags of Bird Island nest late. As late as 14 December, only one of my twenty occupied Gony Ridge nests had eggs. The time of my last visit, 21 December, only two had complete clutches of three eggs, eight had one or two eggs, and the rest were eggless.

I find the late egg dates intriguing. Within our Palmer study plot, an area considerably colder and more hostile than Bird Island, the Antarctic blue-eyed shags (*Phalacrocorax atriceps bransfieldensis*) begin laying in mid-November, fully a month ahead of the Bird Island schedule. One supposes that laying and hatching would occur during a warmer time at Palmer, since the shags hatch naked, without any protective down—a unique condition among Antarctic birds. That region, however, holds far greater advantages to early egg-laying and hatching than first meet the eye. For this and other reasons, I assigned Neil Bernstein, a University of Minnesota graduate student, to my current shag project, which has only recently begun at Palmer.

Not much work has been done on the shags of South Georgia and Bird Island. My British colleagues are quick to admit that these birds have been badly neglected. A most vexing question is why there are so few of them in this region, which easily supports millions of other sea birds. Many unresolved problems surround shags.

Earlier I mentioned the well-known shag behavior of staying put at coastal retreats rather than flying far out to sea. Unlike albatrosses and petrels, shags are not pelagic birds; they exemplify littoral species. No doubt their sedentary behavior was instrumental to the isolation of certain colonies and subsequent evolution of a variety of species or subspecies. The best example of extreme oceanic isolation in shags is found far off the coast of Ecuador, where there exists on the Galapagos Islands the world's only flightless cormorant (*Nannopterum harrisi*).

The sedentary habit poses a pertinent question: How did it happen that shags reached such remote and isolated places as South Georgia and Bird Island? There can be little doubt that shags are strong fliers and capable of sustained flight. The double-crested cormorant (*Phalacrocorax auritus*) regularly migrates in winter from our north central portions of the United States and southern Canada. Year-round resident blue-eyed shags within our Palmer study area fly considerable distances from their rookeries to find open water during periods of unfavorable ice.

Many kinds of birds show up in strange places. South Georgia has recorded a number of vagrant species, but none so strange as that of an egret. According to Peter Prince, and to the amazement of all present at the time, a great egret (*Casmerodius albus*) actually fell dead from the skies over South Georgia. If an egret can make it all the way to that island, there is every reason to believe that under certain circumstances a shag can as well.

Long distance flights may not have been as great in times past. Geologists believe that the coasts of South America were much more extended during the last ice age than they are today; thus flights between South America and the Falkland Islands would have been shorter. Nevertheless, from either South America or the Falklands to South Georgia, flights would have been considerable, even supposing that on the way the birds had stopped at Shag Rocks and other mountain peaks possibly exposed at the time.

Up to now I have said little about these interesting rocks—interesting if only because until recently man has not been able to land on them. Scientists have been able to do little more than speculate as to what they contained and the role they played in such biological conditions as shag distribution and taxonomy. Shag Rocks had their initial impact on me when I discovered them on a map of the Southern Ocean while aboard the *John Biscoe* in 1974. They appeared to be in the middle of nowhere, in the wildest seas imaginable, at 55°33'S, 42°02'W. Presumably they were named for the shags that occupied them; but what were these birds doing there, so far from the nearest land? South Georgia is 240 kilometers to the east, and the Falkland Islands and Tierra del Fuego, 1,110 and 1,500 kilometers, respectively, to the west. With this question in mind, I thumbed through several of the ship's books and journals and quickly found reference to the rocks, though the mystery surrounding them only deepened. Evidently the rocks had been known to explorers, whalers, and sealers for a long time. Rather than places to be exploited, they were to be avoided, for the rugged little mountain peaks spelled disaster for the unwary captain of any ship, large or small.

Shag Rocks are well named; large numbers of shags do indeed occupy the rocks, the highest of which rises about 75 meters above sea level. The turbulent waters all around them accommodate myriads of sea birds, including several species of albatrosses, petrels, and storm petrels. But shags are the birds seen coming off the rocks.

The Swedish Antarctic Expedition of 1901-1903 first reported the presence of this great shag colony. Its failure to obtain specimens presented ornithologists with an unsolved problem that had persisted down to modern times: Which species of shag inhabits Shag Rocks?

A distinguished American ornithologist, Roger Tory Peterson, attempted to unlock the mystery of Shag Rocks and was nearly done in by them. At the time, March 1971, he was a staff lecturer aboard the tourist ship *Lindblad Explorer* on its way to Cape Town from Tierra del Fuego. Accompanying him was the late Robert Cushman Murphy, who had pioneered many oceanic bird studies in these seas.

Peterson's vivid description of Shag Rocks, which I feel needs to be preserved, I quote in part from a letter written to me on 15 August 1975:

As we were approaching South Georgia, still about 200 miles (?) away, we saw in the distance the Shag Rocks, which Murphy told us were among the least visited islands on earth. Few human eyes have ever seen these islands, he said. This interested Lars-Eric Lindblad very much, so Lars ordered the Norwegian captain to drop anchor if he could, or at least to stand by, while we let down one of the lifeboats so that those passengers who were interested could see the rocks at close range. The islands were surrounded by a milling mass of seabirds. It was towards evening. It was a rather sullen sea and the three rocks projected like hag's teeth into the mist. They were literally capped by the low clouds. Their sides were full of shags where they could find places to rest, and the sea seethed with enormous numbers of prions, cape petrels, shags, a few albatrosses, etc. Inasmuch as the sea was somewhat rough, it seemed inadvisable to lower the gangway for boarding the lifeboat. That way, a lifeboat was lowered to deck level and a group of the more adventurous passengers, about 30, crowded into it. Then it was lowered into the sea. We also lowered a zodiac, the rubber landing boat, with Lars Lindblad and Captain Edwin McDonald aboard, and several of the hardcore photographers, which included Lester Peterson, myself and one or two others, transferred into it. We, of course, were able to go closer to the rock than the lifeboat and while we were making our second loop around it (we could not get too close because of the heaving seas that were washing up and down the sides of these black monoliths), the captain started to blow the ship's whistle for us to return. The weather was worsening. Hastening back to the ship, the photographers transferred back to the lifeboat, leaving Captain Mac and Lars Lindblad in the zodiac.

But there were problems in getting the lifeboat back on. The blocks or "cherry pickers" were swinging back and forth, and the problem was to grab one, hold it, and hook it on. Meanwhile, the waves were lifting the lifeboat up and down and I worried about some passenger having his head bashed in by the wildly swinging blocks. I shoved one nice white haired lady rudely to the floor of the boat to save her from such a fate and she immediately got stomach cramps from the excitement (I apologized later). Robert Cushman Murphy, being the experienced one, the old man of the sea, was trying to direct operations. I noticed that he had his hand on the gunwale and would have his fingers crushed next time the lifeboat bumped against the side of the ship. I grabbed his arm and yanked it down quickly, just in time.

There was one good Norwegian seaman who quickly got his block fastened, but the inexperienced Australian boy at the other end had not been in such cold seas before. Lacking mitts, and with hands half frozen, he tried to fasten his end. Finally he did get it fastened and the winch began to lift the lifeboat. At that moment a wave peaked under the boat, and unfastened the block on one end. The other end continued to lift, and passengers in their red parkas started to spill

*down towards the bow which was filling fast with water. My wife,
Barbara, who was in the bow, was up to her waist in cold sea water,
passengers spilling down on her. The deck officers quickly gave orders
to drop the other end of the lifeboat to save us from imminent disaster.*

*At that point one becomes rather philosophical, and I
wondered, well, what next? And I can imagine the thoughts of Lars and
Captain Mac as they bounced around in the zodiac not far away. The
captain then swung the ship, and made a great slick so that there would
be a more tranquil patch of water from which we could lift the lifeboat
without the difficulty we had just experienced. And so it was that we
were finally hoisted back safely.*

*Those passengers who had stayed on deck enjoyed the
action immensely, scarcely realizing the danger that we had been put
to. I, for one, recognized it as one of the more dangerous moments of
my southern adventures. A man does not drown in those cold waters.
He lasts a few minutes and then passes out with shock.*

My first trip to Shag Rocks was as unexpected as the one to South
Georgia earlier. In early December of 1974 Nigel Bonner and I had left the
John Biscoe to join the British naval ship *Endurance* at King Edward
Cove. The *Endurance* was scheduled to sail westward to the Falklands with
the commission to put the first man on Shag Rocks.

British interest in Shag Rocks was not confined to shags. Their geologists and botanists attached great importance to those islands and requested
that rock and plant specimens be collected during the landing if at all
possible. And certainly the British naval personnel had in mind the distinction of another first in far southern exploration.

The *Endurance* departed South Georgia on 4 December and sailed
into the Southern Ocean. Some 14 hours later, on 5 December, she approached the rocks in uncommonly calm seas. Not many birds were about,
except for a few albatrosses and petrels that trailed behind the ship. If the
lack of birds disappointed me, Shag Rocks did not. From afar I saw four
distinct peaks looking much like shark's teeth chewing the sea menacingly.

Despite the calm waters all about the ship, the ocean smashed hard
against the rocks, sending white pillars of water and foam high on the
black cliff walls. A seaman near me remarked that a boat landing there
would be suicidal. The sight held me spellbound until the commotion on
the ship's flight deck quickly snapped me to attention. Naval air crews
were busy securing the rotary blades of a helicopter. Within minutes
Lieutenant Commander Peter Hurst of the Royal Navy and a group of
Royal Marines gyrated out to Shag Rocks in preparation for the first man
landing.

BLUE-EYED SHAGS

To those of us remaining aboard ship, the helicopter looked like a red dot hovering above the distant peaks. According to Hurst, large numbers of shags had peeled off the rocks when the helicopter first approached the peaks, so many in fact that the birds posed a threat to the men's safety. Photographs taken that day disclosed not four but six peaks. At least two of them were connected above waterline.

One group of dislodged shags flying out from the rocks circled close to the *Endurance* and gave me my only good look at the birds. The flight of the shags framed against the distant mountain peaks inspired the watercolor illustration—definitely a first and lasting impression.

Meanwhile storm clouds gathered. The sea heaved and the ship lurched ominously. The helicopter returned briefly to the *Endurance*. Its second flight out succeeded in dropping Lieutenant Simon Hill and several of his Royal Marines on Shag Rocks. From the hovering machine they were lowered on the ends of ropes. Hill later told us that they had hardly any standing room. Shags and their nests hung precariously to narrow ledges and prominences leading down from the top to near the foamy waters below. He looked for but saw no other species of birds.

By the time the landing had been achieved Nigel Bonner and I were suited up and ready to go out to the rocks on a second helicopter. But the seas worsened and an order came down from the bridge to abort the planned flight. The first helicopter was called back. It landed none too soon on a flight deck that began to roll dangerously. The calm had ended and with it all hope for solving the ornithological enigma of Shag Rocks.

Nigel Bonner later confided that he was glad that the Captain had called off our flight. A seal man who spends much of his working hours in boats or on the beaches has little stomach for birds occupying lofty pinnacles. But for a bird man, the order to abandon a once-in-a-lifetime landing was hard to take.

The Royal Marines had brought back a good many rock specimens and some vegetation, taken from shag nests mostly, but not one shag! A few shag eggs tucked in pockets had been smashed beyond description. Although it is a simple matter to grasp an incubating shag by the bill, the problem of holding one struggling and flapping on a mountain peak is too much to ask, even of a Royal Marine.

In rough seas, the *Endurance* left Shag Rocks. Her crew was in high spirits; Captain Noel Bearne and his officers had good reason to be happy over a job well done. At the height of their celebration in the wardroom that evening, Nigel Bonner, sensing my disappointment, vowed to secure shag specimens for me, come what may.

Many weeks later and long after we had parted company, Nigel again

sailed close to Shag Rocks, this time aboard the *John Biscoe*. Captain Phelps dispatched a small boat from which Nigel, assisted by Third Officer Marty Shakesby, shot two shags that flew from the rocks. So far as is known, these were the first shag specimens from Shag Rocks.

Shakesby had seen me remove the skin from a bird carcass only once, but he managed to skin the two shags without further tutoring. The two skins were thoroughly salted, then frozen. Nigel sent them to me via my American colleagues when the *John Biscoe* put in at Palmer Station later that year.

The skins were transported by a United States Coast Guard icebreaker from Palmer to a California Port of Entry and from there they were shipped air express to Minneapolis. I could hardly believe that we possessed such a prize. I handled the skins with reverence, marveling at how those two Fids managed the feat.

The birds taken by Bonner and Shakesby were blue-eyed shags of the *atriceps* type. The salted skins were relaxed, desalted, and made into excellent study specimens, but they lacked some important details. No record had been made of the colors of the legs, feet, webs, eyes, bill, and, especially important in the case of blue-eyed shags, the skin surrounding the eyes and the caruncles. Unlike feathers that retain their natural colors for many years when kept out of sunlight, these fleshy colors fade rapidly, often within hours after death.

An even greater deficiency in the specimen record, the two specimens had not been sexed; so we have no idea of the state of the gonads or sex organs. We can only guess whether the birds were actually breeding on Shag Rocks, or whether they were nonbreeding, perhaps temporary transients, however unlikely.

The enigma of Shag Rocks is far from solved. Known breeding specimens are needed. We also are not certain whether other kinds of shags, not to mention other kinds of birds, breed on Shag Rocks. This much we know: *P. atriceps* occurs there and, judging by the specimens, the Shag Rock birds have a closer affinity to their South American cousins than to those of South Georgia. The latter are noticeably smaller than either South American or Shag Rock birds. Whether the Shag Rock birds are a distinct subspecies, perhaps species, remains to be determined.

CHAPTER 11

Bull fur seal. La Roché peak in far background. Photographed 26 November 1976.

FAREWELL POINT

According to Peter Prince, the western half of Bird Island had the most birds. He was referring to such places as Macaroni Point, Johnson's Cove, Molly Hill, and Pearson's Point. My companions nearly always traveled westward from Lönnberg House, venturing east only when they banded young wanderers and counted seal pups.

I, too, was caught up in the habit of going to the birdy spots in the west. When finally I broke tradition and headed east, I was immediately confronted by Teal Pond and Cobbler's Mound. Always I had a deuce of a time pulling away from those enchanted places. Still I had skuas to count; no doubt there were many of them all the way to Farewell Point at the island's east end.

Peter said that once or twice a season he got out to Farewell; not nearly so many birds were out that way, but the country was rugged and scenic. On 1 December, I set out, not necessarily to go all the way to Farewell, but to go as far as seemed sensible at the time.

I had been on Bird Island a little more than two weeks. During that time I had put to the test every voluntary muscle I possessed. The first days on those dreadful tussock slopes were torturous. I ached all day. I ached in my sleep. In no time, I shed unwanted pounds. The weight that remained, hardened and toughened. By the time I was glancing eastward toward Farewell, I felt wonderfully fit, as well as I had ever been in my life, and probably ever would be.

December 1 was hardly a Bruce Pearson "dingal day." The land was overcast with depressing blankets of wet clouds and the air hung silent and still. Not many wanderers were flying. I purposely took a wide path around Teal Pond and left my heavy tripod near the sooty nests at the gorge by Cobbler's Mound. The prospect was good that the skies would clear enough for photography by the time I returned. After musing about that, I stepped out smartly for unexplored skua country. Some fear the unknown, but for me, exploring new territories brings a good hard-to-describe feeling.

Prince was right: The country to the east was rugged. I had rambled

into a bewildering labyrinth of ridges and deep ravines that required a certain amount of up and down crisscrossing to cover the ground. It is surprising how easy it is to overlook a skua's nest, and I didn't want to miss a single one.

I had not gone far before blundering into fur seals. Some were so high on the slope that I couldn't figure out how they had managed such a high climb in the first place. No longer was I worried about being bitten. I simply followed the rules and never, never trusted to luck. One rule was to look often at the ground immediately ahead—not a bad idea anyway in country enclosed by sea cliffs and sliced by tussock drop-offs; seals added a third dimension.

Several times in high country I had accidentally stepped squarely on a sleeping seal. The furry, rudely awakened, probably was more startled than I; the few seconds it took the sleepy beast to recover was all that I needed to leap to safety. Nonetheless, I experienced a dreadful sensation every time I planted my foot unconsciously on a snoozing fur seal.

Walking the seal-infested slopes of Bird Island can be likened to being interned in a gigantic animal arena. Now I understood how an animal trainer feels surrounded by big cats. Rules are important; one does not ignore them. There is blessed little room for mistake.

Some distance east of Cobbler's Mound, the island's highest mountain rises sharply to 363 meters elevation. Called "la Roché" after the English explorer, the mountain extends one of its several appendage-like ridges a long way to a sea cliff overlooking Bird Sound. When skirting this ridge near its lower end, I passed close to the cliff to enter the country beyond.

I remember the pass well, because it was defended viciously by a pair of skuas. The bold birds gave me such a bad time that I had difficulty locating their nest, which proved to be a spectacular one on a rocky prominence jutting out from the ridge. Marking their eggs was impossible.

At one point I swung my seal club in front of my face to ward off attack. The big bird struck the wood with such force that it spun unconscious to the ground and lay on its back as if in the throes of death—all motionless, legs stiffened and straight up. I thought it surely was dead. I even comtemplated salvaging it for a specimen, but when its legs began to move slowly, I reached down to assist. My reward was a savage bite on the wrist. Any bird that bites that hard isn't bad off, so I left it on its own. Hardly had I started around the ridge when the skua was up and dive-bombing again as if nothing had happened. Typical skua mentality.

On the far side of the ridge I found two skua nests, one that truly puzzled me. Rather than the usual one or two eggs, there were three. Did the female of this nest really lay three eggs, or was the unusual clutch the result of laying by two hens?

It is not unusual for two or more birds of other species to lay in the same nest; certain ducks do so regularly. But highly territorial birds like skuas strongly oppose an intrusion by members of their kind. This paradox demanded an explanation.

Three skuas attending a single nest is highly uncommon or nonexistent at many breeding grounds, but is not all that rare at certain others. Such combinations are referred to in the literature as trios. Nearly all reported trios are brown skuas from islands south of New Zealand, whereas records from South Georgia and the South Orkneys are scarce. One of the best studied cases, however, took place on Bird Island in 1961.

That year Nigel Bonner found a three-egg clutch, which he calls a super-normal clutch, and collected the three attending adults. Although the birds were carefully sexed and found to be one male and two females, the number of ruptured ovarian follicles was not determined for each female. Consequently, we do not know whether the laying was by one or two hens. The trio puzzle is further complicated in that most reported cases involve the normal two-egg clutch. Then, too, some trios consist of two males and one female. Further study of this interesting phenomenon is warranted, but the questions will not be resolved until trios are observed for several seasons within a research area containing marked individuals.

As I stood looking at this super-normal clutch, my first thought was to collect the female for an examination of its ovary. My second thought was that it might be profitable to spend the day watching the nest in the event that three birds were involved in the nesting. My third was foolhardy: I put the investigation off. An inexplicable pull toward Farewell Point proved too much. So off to the east I went, fully satisfied that I would later settle the matter of the three-egg clutch. What a mistake that was—I never got back.

I had not gone far when I descended a steep slope and entered a broad valley with many rocky ridges and prominences. Several shallow streams twisted between them in their rush to the sea. A spectacular sight it surely was, but one that filled me instantly with misgiving.

Seals, seals everywhere, as far as one could see. Up and down the rocky stream beds they went, one long procession after another. Not one prominence was unoccupied in all the valley. If ever a seal haven existed, this was it; and among all those seals, on nearly each of a dozen ridges, roosted a nesting pair of skuas.

For the next two hours I marked eggs, dodging skuas and sidestepping

107

FAREWELL POINT

seals. No two species have worse dispositions. One ugly encounter followed another. What an ordeal! Eventually, I found some much needed relief higher up the valley among a genial group of gentoo penguins standing in one of the streams. The pairs had one or two eggs each in nests of polished stones worn smooth by the cascading waters. Some eggs were barely above the water that flowed all around these strange nests.

Gentoos are the friendliest of penguins. They also are the tidiest in domestic affairs; unlike the big colonizers—the Adélies, chinstraps, and macaronies—that often nest in a sea of guano, which in rainy weather turns into a quagmire of slippery and foul-smelling excrement. All this came to mind as I stood ankle deep in the middle of the stream while taking in the lovely gentoo sight.

Of the many gentoos I had encountered at various places, none had a more efficient system of plumbing, for the rushing waters swept their droppings away. Light rain beginning to fall enhanced the cleanliness and beauty of those immaculate birds. The appealing sight enticed me to walk slowly among them. What balm to my state of mind these attractive, gentle creatures were, after the seal and skua encounters! Before leaving this river colony I had discovered that several gentoos had tiny chicks. Indeed, Bird Island was a gigantic nursery.

Rain mixed with snow began to fall steadily as I passed over a height of ground inhabited by wandering albatrosses. Then I came to the seaward edge of a series of low cliffs and gazed down on a curious rock formation with its center cut through like a doughnut. The Fids called it Natural Arch. To have descended the cliffs for a closer look at the arch would have been suicidal, for the number of fur seals spreading out from there along the beaches was awesome.

The low sea cliffs held another attraction. Cape pigeons nested on ledges near the upper rims in places that were quite accessible, which was not true elsewhere on Bird Island. Peter estimated a hundred breeding pairs for the entire island, and I certainly did not see more. For the second time that day I made tentative plans to return to this general area, to observe the skuas with the three-egg clutch and to photograph the Cape pigeons in fair weather. It was then that I stumbled into *another* skua's nest with a three-egg clutch.

I could hardly believe my eyes. Of literally hundreds of skua nests I had checked during the past several years, none before today held more than two eggs; but in one day I had seen two such nests, only a half kilometer apart. I pondered the situation: Maybe such clutches were not all that uncommon on Bird Island. But those were the last I saw anywhere.

FAREWELL POINT

The fitful half-rain, half-snow so impaired my vision that I feared crossing back through the valley of seals. I already had given up the idea of reaching Farewell Point. My one thought was to get back to high land across that oppressive valley, but every new route I chose was blocked by seals. After endless crisscrossing, backtracking, and circling, I somehow managed not only to traverse the valley unscathed but also marked a couple of skua nests on the way.

Before leaving the valley I had to climb a high, steep bluff where the seals had worn away the tussock. The incline was peppered with white-chinned petrel burrows, and for some reason the birds were outside sitting in the rain on the bare hummocks. Many appeared totally unconcerned by my presence, and I reached down and stroked a few.

Fortunately, not many seals were on the slope this day. I gave wide berth to a couple of hostile young bulls in the hummocks above me. In the unwritten book on fur seals it is forbidden to climb directly below a seal on a steep tussocky slope. Human beings climb slopes faster than seals, but they are no match for the beasts on the downhill stretch. Even the big bulls shoot down the slopes at incredible speeds, seemingly touching only the tops of the slippery hummocks as they go. That same week a big furry had shot past Peter, giving him the scare of his life—and to scare Peter takes some doing.

The hike back to camp along the high route with its few seals was a breeze. Although wet and muddied to the skin, I fairly skipped along the tussock ridges. The weather had turned so foul that by the time Lönnberg House came into view, I was as glad to see it as I had been to leave it some hours before. Even though I had failed to reach Farewell Point, the day had been a good one. My tally for new skua nests that day was twenty-five—not bad by any standard.

December 2 broke clear of rain and snow—some gray swirls in a bit of restless wind, but generally the weather was favorable for locating skua nests. When Peter announced over breakfast that it was time for them to start the annual seal census to the east, I vowed to reach Farewell Point this day.

My plan was to work the upper levels where the skuas occupied a transitional zone between tussock and scree, since I knew from previous experience that the birds favored such areas. Yesterday I had covered the lower and middle zones as far east as Natural Arch. To make the skua count meaningful, I would have to cover the upper zone to the Arch, then all three zones in the unexplored country beyond.

In full stride, I crossed Wanderer Ridge and followed the transitional zone as planned. By the time I reached the big mountain I was forced to follow its arm down to the cliffs of Bird Sound—the same route I had used the day before, where the dive-bombing skua had knocked itself out. Today was no different. The same bird and its mate hurled themselves murderously at me until I was beyond their territory on the other side of the ridge. This time, however, I did not go down into seal valley but, keeping to the transitional zone, ascended the slope instead, thus avoiding the seals.

The ascent east of the ridge was abrupt, leading to an immense rocky jumble that stretched for hundreds of meters. In some places, its stony aprons dipped low toward Seal Valley and then rose again. A number of isolated patches of tussock in the scree all had to be investigated. Skuas abound in such places.

Negotiating the screes upwards, downwards, and crosswise to reach these tussock islands bore fruit: I found nesting skuas everywhere. In crossing certain screes with large, loose rocks, I listened expectantly for the telltale rasping or grating calls of storm petrels, and was disappointed at not hearing one. Much of the rocky rubble seemed ideal for Wilson's storm petrel; also, I was alerted to the possibility of finding the much rarer gray-backed storm petrels that reputedly nest occasionally in scree.

In high country beyond Seal Valley I came to a picturesque alpine lake settled comfortably among lichen-covered scree and scattered clumps of tussock. The last of the high interior snows descended the mountains to this level, lending a touch of elegance to an already lovely scene. At one end of the lake resided a club of seventy-eight docile skuas. Some mildly protested my presence, but most refused to fly far. Ringing the lake were a half dozen nesting skuas that flew off their eggs and came screaming at me.

So captivating was this scene that not even the wicked skuas could hurry me on my way. A few steps beyond the lake was a shallow, pebbly bottomed pool. On its mossy bank stood a stately wandering albatross— a handsome male exquisitely dressed in solid white—that permitted me to approach closely before he plopped his big flat feet into the water and gingerly started across the pond. Halfway across, he stopped, turned and looked back, then plopped on.

The high route was rugged and scenic, nothing short of spectacular. Prince if anything had understated its wild splendor. I found far more birds than expected. Admittedly, all were less accessible than those residing to the west of Lönnberg House; by now I was convinced that the Fids had used good judgment in going west with their routine studies.

FAREWELL POINT

What most surprised me this day was the unexpected appearance of a great macaroni penguin colony stretching from the high screes on which I stood all the way to the sea far below. Nearly all the birds were incubating on an incline so steep that I had to be careful to keep from sliding downhill. I couldn't remember my companions talking about this particular colony, but here it sprawled before me. It was not nearly as large as the one at Macaroni Point; nevertheless, it supported thousands.

I had two choices, either to climb higher and over some uninteresting looking ridges, or to negotiate the steep penguin slope. The latter seemed the wiser choice. I easily accomplished the crossing by running rapidly over the loose, crusty ground, digging my toes in as I went. To hesitate would have meant a long slide down, and an equally long climb up. Although the incline was not dangerous, I hardly relished sliding through a macaroni colony on the seat of my pants.

Not far beyond the penguins I came to the terminal point of a high ridge that ended suddenly in a promontory from which the land descended abruptly to the sea. At the very tip of the promontory was a skua's nest, truly a cliff nest, perched like an eagle's eyrie. The descent along one of the promontory's less formidable sides dropped me into a high basin that led to the island's end. For the first time, Farewell was within reach.

The east end of Bird Island is so irregular that I am not certain which of several points of land I viewed that day was the true Farewell Point. Whatever its geographical location, I spent some exciting hours in its vicinity, exploring the tussocks all the way from the rocky basin screes to the edge of the seas, methodically marking skua nests as I went. My single disappointment was not finding a colony of Antarctic terns on one of the points. Peter Prince thought there might be one out there. The habitat was ideal for terns but there were none this season.

A long, narrow peninsula supported by sheer sea cliffs on three sides definitely was not Farewell Point. Old maps clearly showed it to be Cardno's Point. Whatever its current designation, I found it most attractive, because it had exceptionally luxuriant growths of tussock cut through beneath by innumerable small petrel burrows. I took time off from skua hunting to probe these burrows in hope of establishing new distribution records for Peter. Although I failed to come up with a blue petrel, I did find a Kerguelen diving petrel with an egg—the first reported nesting for the island's eastern extremity.

I also found the season's first newly hatched chicks of the northern giant petrel; a few blue-eyed shags on their then empty nests on cliff ledges below the tussock; a pintail that surely had eggs or chicks that I could not find; small colonies of gray-headed albatrosses; an unbanded young wandering albatross, one of the few overlooked earlier by the Fids; and at long, long last, my first pipit's nest!

I had been struggling chin deep in tussock looking for some unusually well-hidden skua eggs when the little pipit fluttered past my belt buckle. Convinced that it was a genuine nest flush, I stopped searching for the skua nest and painstakingly parted tussock clumps. Soon I zeroed in on four newly hatched pipits, all naked except for fine wisps of down.

The nest of the South Georgia pipit is a large, bulky affair composed of stems and blades of dry tussock. A mass of this plant material often trails down from the bowl-like structure, which itself is snuggly lined with fine tussock strips and fluffy pipit feathers. The whole, including the tail-like appendage, is wedged in the side of a tussock clump, or between clumps, usually well above ground. Always it is covered by a dense canopy of brown and green tussock grass. The clutch is three or four eggs. According to Watson (1975), the only egg described for the species was dull gray-green, thickly speckled and streaked with red-brown. As I saw them, the eggs were of two general types: (1) commonly dull greenish, thickly spotted and blotched with various shades of brown, wreathed or unwreathed, usually with a few sepia or black lines or scrawls principally at the large end; and (2) essentially the same, except that the background is grayish, giving the overall appearance of a brownish rather than greenish egg.

This particular pipit is endemic to the South Georgian region. In the distant past, pipits from South America, perhaps the Falkland Islands, managed a toehold here. Those that clung tenaciously to the land evolved into a unique population of pipits considered by ornithologists to be a distinct species, *Anthus georgica*.

When man and his Norway rats arrived following the region's discovery by Captain Cook, many birds, particularly pipits, suffered enormously. Today, pipits thrive in places not occupied by rats, and perhaps for this reason more than others one can look far and wide for a stray pipit in many parts of South Georgia. On Bird Island where no rats occur, there remains a pipit population conceivably as dense as any in the past.

Magnificent tussock slopes and their thriving summer insect populations are ideal for Bird Island's pipits. The winter scene is quite different. Then the tussock is weighted by thick snows, and the nonmigratory pipits are forced to scratch a meager living in the narrow zone along the icy edge of the beach and open sea. So much is written about the dependence of penguins and petrel-type birds on the sea that it seems strange that not more is said about this little passerine's dependence on the marine environment.

FAREWELL POINT

My British colleagues believe that the pipits' annual mortality in winter is great, but that they overcome such losses through a busy breeding season that starts early and ends late the following summer. The birds appear to be multibrooded, that is, a pair of pipits is capable of producing additional broods after the successful fledging of its first brood. One wonders how many successful broods are produced by a single pair of pipits under optimal conditions.

If the pipits occupied my attention in so spectacular a place as Farewell, they surely must have obsessed me. They did, in fact. I cannot remember during a lifetime of birding having looked so hard for a nest with so little success. Those first couple of weeks on Bird Island were not only frustrating but also depressing with respect to pipits. Try as I might, I had failed repeatedly to come up with a pipit's nest.

Leaving the pipits at Cardno's Point, I returned to the task of finding and recording breeding skuas. Eventually I found the well-hidden nest looked for earlier deep within the tall tussock; another not far from there was on the brink of a sea cliff.

Farewell is Bird Island's remotest and, excepting the sea cliffs, its most inaccessible place. It is also the most scenic because one looks directly across the sound to South Georgia's crystal summits with their purplish cloud formations. In all other directions one views only open sea. It is a bit frightening and unnerving to stand on a tiny island, looking out on seemingly endless waters, and realize that the next land of consequence is a long, long way off. One needs to possess the wings of an albatross to feel secure in viewing such waters. But the land itself, even that as remote as Farewell, inspires in me no pangs of loneliness.

Although I found Farewell to be biologically and aesthetically attractive, common sense tells one that to be caught in such a place in darkness would be anything but pleasant. So, I started back toward the comforts of Lönnberg House, retracing my steps across the macaroni colony, but taking an entirely new direction from that point. Soon I was skirting the upper edge of immense colonies of cliff-nesting black-browed albatrosses. One cannot walk in any direction on Bird Island without being confronted by wildlife, if not by birds, then seals.

By the time I approached the big mountain the weather had turned for the worse. Once again snow and rain obscured my view, as it had the day before. Nonetheless, I marked forty-two new skua nests, this, by far, the best day; and ensconced in those skua hills and ravines was still another young wanderer without a band. I had much to talk about at Lönnberg House that evening.

Some days afield are good, some bad. Field biologists accept both.

114   *South Georgia pipit at its nest in tussock. Produced from an ink drawing.*

That day out to Farewell and back held more memories for me than usual. Topping the perfect day was the finding of my second pipit's nest—this one with three eggs neatly hidden in a tussock bank not far from Cobbler's Mound.

A pipit's nest, even a South Georgia one, is not all that hard to find. I cannot understand why it took me so long to find my first. I suspect that like breaking in one's muscles for the arduous task of negotiating tussocks, so through usage, one's vision and hearing become acute and sensitive to the environment. In becoming accustomed to tussock one also becomes accustomed to pipit signs—a sudden flash or whirring of feather, a peeping of young, an adult flying with an insect. One even becomes knowledgeable about what constitutes good, marginal, and poor habitat for a given species. Toward the end of my stay on Bird Island, I could predict where the next pipit's nest would be. After awhile one could become a proficient predator. Whatever the reasons, following my pipit day near Farewell Point, I came close to averaging a new pipit's nest daily for the remainder of my tenure on Bird Island.

One of these nests held my attention because the attending adult, believed to be the female, was so tame that within arm's length it fed its four young great beakfuls of larval and adult insects. Since its nest was in the vicinity of my favorite blue petrel and molly patches near Macaroni Point, I visited the site time and again, the result being a drawing of this bird perched on lithe tussock stems.

The drawing of the bird beside its nest and eggs had its conceptual beginning high on Wanderer Ridge, not far from Teal Pond. The parent bird was not at all tame, but its nest with the pendulous mass of fibrous tussock was attractive and typical. A few atypical nests, including one close to the ground in stunted tussock and another found by Bruce Pearson in a great mat of moss, I wanted to sketch as well but was pressed for time before my departure. I would have liked nothing better than to have launched a study of the South Georgia pipit that memorable day near Farewell Point, had it not been for the skuas—who kept me fully occupied.

South Georgia pipit clinging to lithe tussock stems. Produced from a watercolor.

115

CHAPTER 12

Pair of brown skuas. Photographed in North Valley on 20 November 1976.

SKUAS

Skuas are fierce predatory and piratical sea birds belonging to the small bipolar family Stercorariidae that is related to gulls and terns. Three widely dispersed Arctic skuas are known to Americans as jaegers. Although they have confusing light, intermediate, and dark color phases, the adults of each of the three species can be readily identified in the field by their respective elongated central tail feathers, or rectrices. A fourth species, known widely as the great skua, is classified either with the jaegers in the genus *Stercorarius* or in the separate genus *Catharacta*, but is recognized by all as the species *skua*. In the Northern Hemisphere, the great skua has a rather restricted breeding range confined to Iceland, the Faeroes, and Scotland, including the Orkneys and the Shetlands.

These same great skuas, or closely related ones, are circumpolar in the far south. Regardless of one's taxonomic preference, all are heavy-bodied and resemble in size and shape a medium to large-sized gull. All have powerful, black, hooked bills; heavy, black legs and feet with webbed toes that have short but strong claws; fairly short tails lacking the greatly elongated central rectrices of jaegers; and large wings with prominent white quill patches that flash.

A peculiar behavior common to skuas is ground flashing—a showy display given by paired birds, often simultaneously, on the nesting territory. A standing pair of skuas will throw their outstretched wings above their back, tilt their heads, and call raucously before a trespassing individual. The white flashing is conspicuous, the calls harsh and unpleasant. If these signals fail to stop an intruder, the birds resort to an effective harassing behavior that I shall later describe in bloody detail.

The plumage of skuas is brownish, more or less mottled or streaked with gray, buff, or cinnamon. Some South American skuas have attractive bright cinnamon patches. The collars of many breeding individuals show golden streaks called hackles. Even so, the skua is no beauty. The least handsome are those that occupy Bird Island and many other islands in the Southern Ocean surrounding Antarctica. These are the brown skuas, classified by some ornithologists as a separate species, *Catharacta lonnbergi.* The skuas of South America, Falklands, Tristan da Cunha, and Iceland are closely related to these brown skuas, but our taxonomists are uncertain whether we are dealing with full species or merely subspecies. One thing is certain. The brown skuas of Bird Island are big, ugly, and tough.

The south polar skua (*Catharacta maccormicki*), also known as Maccormick's skua, is least like the others. It breeds all around continental Antarctica and adjacent islands, and is the only bird recorded for the South Pole and actually seen there by Beatrice Axelrod, one of our University of Minnesota students. South polar skuas can be separated from the other skuas in the field by their smaller size, including bills and legs, and many have conspicuous pale heads and necks. Those of the Antarctic Peninsula region are, however, predominantly dark plumaged, therefore easily mistaken at a distance for other skuas.

Brown skuas are extending their breeding ranges southward along the Antarctic Peninsula, where in recent times they have come in contact with breeding south polar skuas. Our Palmer study area lies within this narrow range of overlap. I was intrigued by the finding that two distinct skuas occupied a common breeding ground at Palmer, for here was an unexcelled opportunity to observe the ecology and behavior of the two under identical environmental conditions. Since they interbreed to some extent, the resulting hybrids added another dimension. As soon as it was feasible, I put David R. Neilson, one of my graduate students, on the skua project, while later assigning another, Pamela Pietz, to a different phase of the same project.

However attractive the Palmer study area, in the back of our minds was the nagging fear concerning the skua project: Was the influence of one species on the other giving us a distorted picture? Bird Island provided the means of observing skuas on a breeding ground where no overlap exists because, so far as I know, the British have no south polar skua records for either South Georgia or Bird Island. The brown skuas of Bird Island are relatively free from south polar skua influences, genetic or otherwise.

Bird Island was attractive for still another reason. During my brief visit to the island with Nigel Bonner in 1974, I was impressed by the large numbers of breeding brown skuas. As much as I wanted to see the wanderers, blue petrels, pintails, and pipits, the skuas have always been the number one attraction, and they still are.

Why this strong attraction for a bird not especially endowed with beauty, intelligence, or a genteel disposition? My reasoning is simple: I find the biological problems posed by skuas really exciting. The birds lend themselves exceptionally well to field observation and techniques. For example, the dive-bombing behavior referred to so often enables one to

catch the birds easily; and only after capture can birds be banded and color-coded individually for convenient and positive field identification.

How does one catch a dive-bombing skua? Simply, in a big fish net thrust suddenly in the path of the diving bird as it approaches one's head. Since skuas often attack from the rear, one soon becomes deft at spinning around at the last moment to catch the individual before it veers off. One also discovers that a netted skua is a tough customer. I soon learned to wrap the bird's wings and upper legs in a makeshift straight jacket to measure the bill and tarsi before banding. Even so, a good netting session was invariably painful.

The skua's hooked bill is a terrible weapon, but a dive-bombing individual usually strikes first with its strong feet and toenails and occasionally whacks one hard with its wings. A captured skua is worth the resulting black and blue punishment, however, because a field biologists's first objective usually is to mark as many subjects as feasible in the study area.

Newly arrived skuas are not aggressive when occupying their traditional nesting territories in spring, which in the Southern Hemisphere begins in late October. Slowly at first, but steadily day by day, the level of aggression rises perceptibly in these birds, in response to changes in hormonal levels. By the time eggs appear, the skuas are poised to spring at all intruders from high perches overlooking their territories. In defense of eggs or chicks, they attack trespassing humans, skuas, almost anything, with a vengeance.

The Bird Island skuas defend territories from near the beaches all the way to the barren slopes of the high interior. Some even occupy ledges on the precipitous sides of mighty Tonk. Believe me, a screaming skua careening down a mountainside toward one's head is a skua to be avoided. It could easily remove one's scalp or knock one off the cliff.

Those skuas occupying the lower levels of Bird Island launch ground

South polar skua. Photographed by the author in the vicinity of Palmer Station near the Antarctic Peninsula on 20 January 1975.

119

attacks in addition to the more conventional aerial ones. They fling themselves directly at an intruder from a standing position on the ground—a most unusual tactic that I had not seen outside the Bird Island breeding grounds. It appears to be a defense against the hordes of seals that occupy the island's lower areas. In such places, one often sees a nesting skua leap from the ground to turn aside a seal or one of the big wanderers.

I had hoped to achieve a number of objectives with the Bird Island skuas, one being simply a nest count for Peter Prince. He felt that either earlier estimates were inaccurate or breeding populations of skuas had increased in recent times. I was convinced that many more skuas nested on Bird Island than formerly believed; obtaining an accurate count was another matter.

Not that a skua's nest is all that difficult to find. The dive-bombing birds quickly disclose a nest's location. The closer one is to the eggs or chicks, the more intense the attacks. One plays a game of hot and cold with skuas. Their usual two eggs are easy enough to spot in the scantily lined scrape in bare or mossy ground, but the difficulty is that egg laying in skuas is spread over a long period. New territories and fresh eggs keep popping up, even in areas long occupied by birds incubating eggs or brooding chicks. We have found little evidence that these late nestings are attempts at replacing lost clutches.

To check an area only once for nests is not enough. I was not able to return often enough to the many breeding areas on rugged Bird Island with its complex system of ridges, ravines, steep slopes, and dense growths of tussock. Even so, I marked upwards of 300 skua nests—a hundred more than Peter had expected me to find. I continued to find fresh eggs until the time of my departure and would have found considerably more had I been on the island a few weeks longer. In the Palmer area, the skuas also show an asynchronous egg-laying schedule, whereas the gulls occupying breeding grounds close by have a highly synchronous one. We cannot help but wonder why the skuas are so unstructured in their egg-laying times.

One Bird Island behavior I didn't count on was that of incubating skuas that were prone to remain silent on nests concealed by tussock. These individuals were easily overlooked in areas where the population was dense, for several skuas in the air at once can be distracting. On occasion I walked close to an incubating skua without seeing it, but a short time later, on backtracking through the same area, I flushed it. Those close sitters were so reluctant to fly that they often remained on their eggs and pecked at my Wellingtons.

I cannot even estimate how many close sitters went undetected, but it may have been considerable, judging by our Lönnberg House skuas, George and Mavis. Although their territorial boundaries were not rigidly defined in the area immediately surrounding the building, the two of

Brown skua set to launch a "ground attack" on a wandering albatross in the vicinity of the skua's nest. Attack shown on facing page. Photographed near Teal Pond on 3 December 1976.

120

them generally occupied the beach side of the hut, and another pair the opposite side.

In the beginning I mistook our banded George for Mavis. This mix-up wouldn't have happened if I had seen the pair side by side, for in skuas there is a slight sexual dimorphism, females on the average being larger. Mavis was considerably larger than George. That I didn't see the two together was in itself a clue that they may have had a nest nearby. My colleagues, however, insisted that the pair always nested on the exposed stream flats close by. Peter even showed me several fresh nest scrapes in scattered patches of badly worn tussock.

The clincher came when John said that even though Mavis was not producing eggs this year, she had contributed a fair share of genes during her long life, implying that Mavis was now too old to produce eggs, though her precise age was not known. At that point I conceded. It certainly seemed as though George and Mavis were not doing much for the skua gene pool that season.

The same could be said of the other pair, the unnamed skuas at Lönnberg House. Like neighboring George and Mavis, the only thing they produced was a couple of empty scrapes. Or so it seemed.

As late as 8 December, I caught a glimpse of sly old George coming off a tussock bank just up from Lönnberg House. On investigating, I soon found Mavis' secret well-hidden in the tussocks. She was so reluctant to flush that I had to pry her off the nest to see the eggs. And when I did, she bit me hard. She actually bit me, good friends that we were! The worst part of finding Mavis' nest was that it proved embarassingly close to the stream bed that all of us used daily in going to and from North Valley. To make matters worse, we had in the meanwhile found the nest of the other pair of Lönnberg House skuas, also secluded in dense tussock not far away.

The first egg of Mavis' clutch hatched on 12 December. Although I had recorded my first skua chick of the season as early as 2 December, our pet skuas were among the earliest to nest and must have been incubating at the time of my arrival on 14 November. Mavis' second chick hatched about two days after the first, but not much hope was given for its survival or, for that matter, that of its older sibling. According to my companions, old George and Mavis had failed miserably at chick rearing during the past season or two.

As secretive as some skuas surely are, the large majority are not. Most skuas advertise their intentions. They explode like dynamite on wings.

How well I learned that lesson far up the tussocky side of Tonk, on a fine Thanksgiving Day. As usual, I knelt beside the skua's nest while marking each egg with an indelible number. Before doing so I had intentionally placed one end of my seal club well above my head, since skuas usually aim at the highest point, be it scalp, hat, or club.

Incubating brown skua in dense tussock. Photographed by the author during a landing on Albatross Islet in The Bay of Iles, South Georgia on 15 November 1974.

Incubating brown skua in sparse tussock. Photographed in North Valley following a summer snow storm on 9 December 1976.

Of the two skuas diving at me then, I didn't see the one coming in fast and low to my left. Instead of striking the tip of my club, for some reason it flew into the side of my head and drove the ax handle hard against my cheek. I was smacked flat. The egg in my hand popped. The skua lay motionless on the ground beside me.

I lay stunned, unable to comprehend at first what had happened. About the time I picked myself up, cursing at having broken the egg, the also stunned skua miraculously recovered, hobbled a short distance, and flew off.

Back at Lönnberg House my cheek swelled to unbelievable dimensions, and the pain was fierce. It seemed certain that two of my upper molars were loose. The only thing that kept me on top of things that evening was the responsibility of having to cook an American Thanksgiving dinner for my British friends. I had no turkey to serve them, only a canned ham ringed with pineapple. I would gladly have roasted a skua!

Skuas are determinate layers, that is, these birds almost always lay a clutch of two eggs rather than an undetermined number. Although sometimes only a single egg is laid, one should look carefully for a second egg that may have been dislodged from the shallow nest because, as on Bird Island especially, an egg can roll a long way on a steep decline. Even the egg that rolls only a few centimeters is an abandoned egg. Skuas make no attempt to retrieve it. One would think that it would be a simple matter for the parent to push the egg back in the nest with bill or foot, but evidently this seldom, if ever, takes place in the world of skuas.

When two siblings hatch, often only one of them, usually the older one, survives to fledging. There is good evidence that survival rates of this kind relate to food abundance, for when food is hard to come by, the younger sibling is underfed and often perishes. On the other hand, both siblings may fledge when food is abundant and available.

David Neilson and I were amazed to find extraordinarily high survival rates among our south polar skuas at Palmer. We attributed their success to the area's food-rich seas, which at times abound in krill and fish, the principal diet of these birds. The brown skuas breeding close by had quite a different food fare in that they fed chiefly on eggs and chicks gleaned from the Adélie penguin rookeries that they patrolled. This seemingly cruel predation in itself is of vital importance to penguin productivity, because if it were not for these territorial brown skuas, the large numbers of surplus predators in having no controls would soon create mayhem. The territorial brown skuas spend considerable time and energy driving off the surplus predators. Compared with the price the colony would pay otherwise, the cost for this kind of watchdog service is relatively slight: a few of their eggs and chicks. No free living is possible on this earth, even in the remote world of penguins.

The rigid partitioning of the area's food resources was not apparent to us at first, because both south polar and brown skuas are predators and scavengers of renown. Certain specialists or rogues among the south polar skuas were expert at picking off particular prey, such as tern eggs and chicks, and predation of this sort is conspicuous. Whenever the Palmer Station cooks waved food scraps in the air, the skuas immediately flew in from the nesting ridges, from as far as a half kilometer away. Since artificial feedings introduced a serious bias in our skua studies, we stopped the feedings, closed the open dumps, and put food scraps that could not be burned in metal drums to be hauled away later by ships.

The high productivity of south polar skuas continued unabated until the crash came. And what a crash! Productivity of chicks fell precipitously. Late summer storms had prevented the adults from foraging at sea efficiently; their krill and fish take was not enough to feed the chicks, which slowly starved. The following austral summer was a disaster for many birds at Palmer. Pack ice jammed the seas around the nesting grounds and remained fast against the shores throughout the breeding season. The south polar skuas defended territories, but had to abandon them periodically to forage elsewhere, when presumably they flew a long way to open water areas. Invariably they returned to their defended but chickless breeding spots.

A few south polar skuas did lay eggs but these were abandoned before hatching. Another surface feeder, the Antarctic tern, simply dropped its eggs on the Palmer breeding grounds and made no attempt to incubate them. Dominican gulls had so much trouble in obtaining fish and limpets that their chicks starved one by one. Species that regularly dive and swim underwater for their prey bred successfully, including blue-eyed shags and the many Adélie penguins. The penguin-dependent brown skuas also had high chick production!

David Neilson was interested particularly in cross matings of the two skua species and had an unusual opportunity to see how the adverse ice conditions influenced the breeding of mixed pairs. The pairs simply didn't form. No hybrids were produced. Neilson attributed the failure to the male south polar skua's inability to forage properly and obtain enough food to establish a strong bond with the female brown skua (the male south polar skua usually mates with a female brown skua). Severe ice conditions inhibit cross matings and help to maintain the integrity of the species.

The brown skuas of Bird Island neither suffered from excessive ice nor a lack of food during my visit. Some of them laid claim to the penguin rookeries, but it seemed to me that many, perhaps the majority, fed on

123

seal carcasses when available. Even those birds nesting in the high interior wore incriminating blood smears on the base of their bills and foreheads, though these stains were not nearly as obvious as those that brightened the heads of northern giant petrels.

On the fur seal beaches, the gorging on carcasses was hardly inconspicuous. Both skuas and giant petrels often engaged in loud, frenzied squabbles over the bodies of newly born seal pups. One day I noted no less than eight skuas and a giant petrel fighting furiously over one tiny pup. Peter Prince claimed that he could always tell when the predators had one. Indeed he could, not only by the unusually loud ruckus, but also by the birds' peculiar flapping movements. Jumping up and down and flailing one another with outstretched wings, they created the odd illusion of puffs of smoke rising from the masses of seals.

Scattered among the Bird Island skuas were specialists that preyed heavily on specific kinds of birds other than penguins. Judging by the remains found near certain skua nests, the Antarctic prion was hit the hardest, followed by blue petrels and Kerguelen diving petrels. At a single skua site I counted the remains of thirty-two prions and one diver. All the carcasses were scattered within three meters of the nest, but not all had been eaten, many not even partly eaten.

This stockpiling of food near the nest reminded me of the accumulation of uneaten lemming carcasses at snowy owl (*Nyctea scandiaca*) nests in the Canadian Arctic. The hoarding is indicative of a bountiful food supply, whatever its true function.

These "petrel specialists" become adept at patrolling the tussock corridors, for I found a good many kills even in the dense growths. Like Tolkien's giant spiders, the skuas lie poised in the corridors and await the arrival of innocent prions. The burrowing petrels are cushioned against predation of this type, for in many places they do not normally fly from the sea to their burrows except at night. Some petrels refuse to return to their burrows even in moonlight, so there must be high survival value in the evolution of such behavior. Skuas obviously catch some of them despite those countermeasures, probably because they have learned to hunt during the short polar night as well as during the long daylight hours.

Peter Prince is one of the few who have studied predatory-prey relations of this sort. He obtained quantitative information on the various age groups of blue petrels being preyed on at Pearson Point. By placing mist nets near his study burrows, he came up with all sorts of surprises and intriguing questions on blue petrel predation. We will have to await publication of his study for the details.

The more I observe predatory birds the more I appreciate how individuals vary in their skills and techniques. The brown skuas of Palmer appear to be tied so closely to the penguin rookeries that we have not noticed much variation in their food preferences. South polar skuas definitely have rogues within their ranks.

We believed that the continued predation of an Antarctic tern colony was due to a flock of skuas that resided near Palmer Station, since a steady stream of these birds could be seen flying over the ternery almost any hour. However, a subsequent study disclosed that a single pair of skuas nesting close by accounted for most of the killings. The numbered bird bands that we had placed on the baby terns showed up in the same skua's nest time and again. We had a similar experience at still another ternery.

These observations do not imply that these rogues live entirely on terns. The limited amount of protein derived from a small tern colony of a dozen or so pairs hardly supports a family of skua. The main source of the rogue's food is still the sea, krill and fish remaining the staple items. Tern eggs and chicks give the skuas an occasional treat—a bit of frosting on the cake, nothing more.

Insignificant as the tern egg or chick is to the marauding skua, some tern colonies can be destroyed by a clever skua. Somehow the abundant Antarctic terns at Palmer survive the onslaught. They have adapted to the point where they are among the first of the south polar birds to lay their eggs, whereas terns elsewhere in the world, including the Arctic, are notoriously late nesters. The Palmer terns nest so early that some of their young are flying before the first skua young hatch. For these terns early nesting and consequent early fledging is advantageous, because after the skua young hatch, predation of tern nests rises perceptibly. Antarctic terns are also persistent nesters. A pair having lost a set of eggs quickly abandons the original breeding colony and flies off and joins another some distance away, where nesting is repeated.

I did not determine whether the brown skuas of Bird Island forage at sea for food. My stay on Bird Island was much too brief to study the feedings of chicks. Had that been possible, I would have located special territories to observe the chicks apart from concealing vegetation. I did, in fact, locate ideal study territories well above Wanderer Ridge, in alpine meadows with tussock so thin that a chick could not hide for long. Should some investigator return to Bird Island with a food-oriented study in mind, I know exactly where to send the person. The first season afield often is a reconnaissance.

Despite the shortcomings, I gained a wealth of information on brown skuas. I left Bird Island convinced that when food is abundant and available, these birds raise both siblings of a nesting to fledging. Before leaving I had seen quite a few sibling chicks scrambling about. By then a few from early nestings were well on their way to fledging.

Peter insisted that the Bird Island skuas refused to swim at sea, or for that matter, in fresh water pools. I have to admit that I never saw one swimming. Standing in shallow water, yes, but swimming, no. I have since seen the Chilean skua (*Catharacta skua chilensis*) of Tierra del Fuego swimming at sea both near and far from shore and, on a number of occasions, watched the south polar skuas swimming while foraging far at sea.

Whether or not the Bird Island skuas swim, they love to stand in shallow water. One day I deepened a spot in a creek bed of the stream that flowed by the front lawn of Lönnberg House. My purpose was to have a place deep enough to wash the mud from my Wellingtons. Old George was on hand to take in the activity. No sooner had I stepped out of the creek when he jumped in, and from then on the little depression in the creek bed became George's special bath, where, belly deep in water each day, he whipped his feathers and splashed vigorously. The depression kept silting in, so that I had to scrape it clean rather often, and always I did so under the critical eye of George.

An important skua objective of mine was to see whether any of the Bird Island pairs bred in dense concentrations. Since numbers of brown skuas at Palmer are more or less dependent on the number of penguins, particularly on the number of available territories adjacent or near the penguin rookeries, the birds are rather widely dispersed. A few are somewhat concentrated in one island area but they keep a healthy distance apart while partitioning the penguin food stocks.

Whether the brown skuas breeding independently of penguins ever concentrated their nestings was a question foremost in my mind. The answer was apparent: They most certainly did, at least on Bird Island, where their concentrations were as dense as any of those of the south polar skuas we saw in the Palmer area. In both places, some skua nests were only 15 to 20 meters apart!

Shrunken territories of such fierce predatory birds are truly remarkable, considering how aggressive skuas are to trespassing members of their kind. No matter how small or large the territory, it is defended to the utmost. No eggs or chicks are left unattended. While one parent is off feeding, the other remains with the clutch or brood. Chases are common in skua country. When swift flying skuas meet head-on above a territorial boundary, more often than not they veer off sharply rather than cross the crucial line.

Crossing the line can be fatal. Typical are the invisible but extant lines of demarcation in our famous "Skua Alley" near Palmer Station. This hideous place is a deep, narrrow passage between two rock walls on one of Palmer's many offshore islands. Walking down the corridor, one is continually bombarded by dive-bombing skuas; there is no escaping them. Trespassing skuas fare even worse—judging by the number of dead or crippled birds found there some years.

Of special interest are the skua "clubs," composed of a few to as many as a hundred or more individuals that regularly occupy favored loafing grounds. Mentioned earlier were one at Flagstone Pond and another in a boggy depression near Macaroni Point. Others were situated near the rim of the precipitous sea cliff backing North Valley and at a high alpine lake near the eastern side of the island. Immediately adjacent to all these loafing grounds were concentrations of nesting skuas, and the numbers of skua nests increased as the season advanced. The late nesters wedged their way into what appeared to be a popular skua nesting habitat at the edge of an equally popular loafing ground.

A skua club, according to R. P. Schlatter, an ornithologist fron Valdivia, Chile, is "a social aggregation composed mainly of nonbreeding individuals during the breeding season, assembled in a traditional area and away from or adjacent to other terrestrial breeding birds. Most of the individuals in the clubs are derived from the nearby breeding colony and will eventually breed there." At first, I believed that clubs in the vicinity of Palmer Station consisted entirely of young nonbreeding birds, since under normal conditions skuas usually require four years and often five or more years before attaining sexual maturity. This is a wrong assumption. Our banded adults from marked nests dispelled any doubt as to whether breeding birds participate in club activities, a fact also appreciated by Schlatter, who noted nesting birds in one of the clubs he studied in the Ross Sea area of Antarctica. Nevertheless, it appears to me that on Bird Island the breeders and nonbreeders mingle more than they do in the Palmer and Ross Sea areas. But wherever you find skuas, individuals on the club premises are always friendlier and more congenial than those occupying nesting territories.

The migratory habits of brown skuas remain a mystery. We know that most if not all migrate from the breeding grounds of the Falkland Islands, South Georgia, Bird Island, the South Orkneys, the South Shetlands, and the Antarctic Peninsula. All are thought to fly to the coasts of South America, but for lack of banding returns, we cannot say positively. The chance recovery of a banded bird is slight, especially for one far from the place of banding. Often the bands wear so thin that even after a few season's wear, the numbers cannot be read.

My British companions conceded that of the many bands being carried by the Bird Island skuas not one is legible. Over the years all have been worn smooth. Even old George sports a numberless band. How nice it would be to have George's history. Was he banded as an adult, or as a chick of known age? Perhaps he came from a nest close to Lönnberg House? Alas, we shall never know.

The problem of band deterioration is so serious that we currently obtain our bands from C. G. Ohman & Son of S-56023 Bankeryd, Sweden, who are skilled in etching numbers in a tough metal highly resistant to abrasion and corrosion. The United States banding program supplies the identifications and series of numbers. Despite these problems, our Palmer-banded south polar skuas have been recovered in remarkable places. We have, in fact, another bipolar migrant.

You may recall that the Arctic tern (*Sterna paradisaea*) has long been known to have a spectacular migration that takes it from one polar region to the other and back again in the course of a year; that the species probably enjoys more daylight hours than most other life forms; that many of its young probably circumnavigate Antarctica before returning to traditional northern breeding grounds when two or more years old. But a skua?

Consider the evidence. A south polar skua egg marked by David Neilson near Palmer Station in December hatched the following January and the chick was banded by him later that month. Neilson last saw the chick on 20 February, not long before he thought it fledged. Since most adult and young skuas left the breeding ground in April, it was probably among the majority that departed then, for we have few skua records for May and none for June.

The precise departure date for the chick of known age and parentage seems minor enough; but this chick was taken by an Eskimo at Godthabsf Jordan, Greenland, the following 31 July. Within a span of three or four months, this youngster had flown a minimum of 14,400 kilometers—if it had flown in a straight line, which almost certainly it had not. Finn Salomonsen, the Danish ornithologist, reported the recovery and claimed that it was the longest flight of any banded bird on record. Well might it be. It certainly was one heck of a flight for a baby skua.

Some will argue that the long flight was a fluke—that the bird was a vagrant blown off course by the winds. We may have thought the same, were it not for the startling revelation that close at hand was still another Greenland specimen of south polar skua.

This unbanded specimen had been around for a long time— since July of 1902, in fact, when taken at Ujarasugssuk, Greenland. It had been kept in a Copenhagen museum, where it lay overlooked and labeled as one of many great skua (*Catharacta skua skua*) specimens from the breeding birds of Iceland and islands north of Scotland, until recently, when it was reclassified by Pierre Devillers, the Belgian ornithologist.

Finn Salomonsen showed me the 1902 specimen: It is a dark plumaged skua typical of the Antarctic Peninsula birds; it could easily have originated at Palmer. Meanwhile, more returns from David Neilson's Palmer-banded south polar skuas kept coming in: one from Baja California, Mexico, on the Pacific Coast, and three separate returns from Brazil on the Atlantic side. New information also came to light on the misidentification of old south polar skua specimens from the State of Washington, and recently a south polar skua specimen was taken on the coast of North Carolina. All these records confirm a growing suspicion that former reported sightings of skuas off both coasts of North America are suspect, for no longer can we assume that a skua flying near the coasts of North America is readily referable to the Iceland or South American birds. There is a better than even chance that it will turn out to be a south polar skua!

Added to this growing accumulation of evidence are the authenticated sightings of south polar skua off the seas of Japan. These birds come from another region of Antarctica, most likely the Ross Sea area. We feel certain that our birds fly from Palmer directly across the Drake Passage, where we actually have seen migrating skuas from ships. Once the skuas reach South America, we believe that they fly northward along the Atlantic and Pacific coasts of the Americas.

It is our fondest dream to place radio transmitters on some of our skuas and, with the help of satellites, track them along their lengthy migration routes. This arrangement would provide precise times and locations of our migrating birds.

Electronic engineers at the University of Minnesota have pioneered in developing new techniques in radio telemetry. We hope for even greater advancements in this area. With satellite tracking will come a new frontier in tracing migratory patterns. But this is for another time and another writing. Suffice it to say that there are many unanswered questions concerning skuas. One cannot learn much about a species during a lifetime, let alone a few seasons afield.

Earlier I said that Professor George Miksch Sutton's first lesson in field biology concerned safety. His second lesson was to get into the field often—as often as humanly possible. That is the starting line; that is where the action is—and the excitement. It is hard work, but it pays off in the contribution one makes to knowledge.

Sutton's third important lesson is that field data, by and large, come in bits and pieces. True; how many times have I had to be content with dabs of information! But the challenge and fun has been trying to put all of the parts in place—even when it means scrambling the pieces of the puzzle repeatedly for a clean start and a new hypothesis.

One little piece of the Bird Island puzzle, insignificant in itself, but so very important to me, was the outcome of George and Mavis' offspring. The siblings were still downy when I left the island at a time when their survival was in doubt.

Months later, news of their fate arrived from abroad. According to John Croxall, the babies survived! Both of them fledged! George and Mavis, my hat is off to you, wherever you may be this moment.

CHAPTER 13

King penguins on a gravel bar in the mouth of the Penguin River
at Hestesletten, South Georgia. Photographed on 24 December 1976.

LAST IMPRESSIONS

December 21, my last day on Bird Island, was cold and dominated by snow showers, interspersed with brief moments of intense sunshine. In early morning I started out for Molly Ridge in search of the season's first molly chicks, thinking all the while that I had at least a day to complete unfinished business before the arrival of *Endurance's* helicopter. The truth was that I had less than eight hours remaining, for the helicopter arrived sooner than scheduled.

With the finding of a gray-headed chick, I closed the chapter on albatrosses. Since I had several important skua nests to check in North Valley, I started back earlier than usual and unexpectedly ran into Peter Prince in the lower tussocks of Molly Hill. I particularly enjoyed the walk back to Lönnberg House with Peter. His companionship was always a treat and this day the more so. As we made our way down through some tall tussock of a steep decline, he said that we would be returning by way of Square Pond—that notorious seal-favored lowland I had been forbidden to visit alone.

Square Pond was the last major area of Bird Island left for me to see, and I particularly wanted to record its nesting pairs of skuas. These proved surprisingly few, though the seals were everything that the Fids had claimed. The pond itself had less appeal than those of the high interior, perhaps because the vegetation on its banks had been mutilated by the seals. Pretty or not, the pond could boast of having been the site of a rare vagrant bird seen earlier that spring. On one of its muddy aprons Peter and others had observed a white-rumped sandpiper—that little peep of a shorebird that is so much at home in Canada's northern tundra.

A dignified small colony of gentoo penguins inhabited the outskirts of Square Pond. Conspicuous markers by some of the nest mounds advertised the scientific activities of my British colleagues. Despite the tattered condition of the vegetation, the nesting ground in the tussock reminded me of those gentoo colonies I had visited much earlier on South Georgia at Cooper Bay. Very different in appearance were the Bird Island colonies

Gentoo penguin with its two chicks on nest of tussock. Photographed by the author at Cooper Bay, South Georgia, 14 December 1974.

on the coastal flats of Johnson Cove and tumbling mountain brooks of Seal Valley. Some fairly large gentoo chicks, two to a nest as a rule, groped clumsily at the feet of an attendant parent.

On leaving Square Pond and its gentoo inhabitants, we made our way slowly back to camp, encountering relatively few seals on the steep slopes overlooking Jordan Cove's crowded beaches. More excitement and commotion than usual greeted us when we arrived at Lönnberg House. We learned from John and Bruce that the helicopter would arrive within an hour to drop my replacement off and take me out to the *Endurance*. The next hour was pandemonium. I threw everything I had into several duffle bags, wrapped preserved bird specimens as best I could, paid John for film he had obtained for me earlier, and somehow managed to pack frozen bird specimens in a special box provided by Bruce. I left behind with Peter a bulky tripod that I could not wedge in anywhere.

Under the whirling drone of an approaching helicopter, a moving farewell took place on the porch of Lönnberg House. Each of my companions shook my hand firmly and bade me a friendly goodby. Then Bruce presented me with a lovely painting—one I had seen evolve and had admired so much—depicting explicitly that marvelous invasion of petrels that foggy night at the time of my arrival. I treasure Bruce Pearson's "A Night on Bird Island. The Kitchen Window," because it captures so vividly all the emotion and fond memories.

Bruce also gave me another painting, this one a quick sketch of the camp skuas, George and Mavis, a happy reminder that in my confusion I

132

King Penguin

Gentoo Penguin

Macaroni Penguin

Antarctic Fur Seal

had reversed their roles on making their acquaintance. This charming painting was to have been the centerpiece at a farewell celebration that evening. My premature departure deprived me of the delectable Stanley greyhounds and a last chance to even the score at Ukkers; but the centerpiece I could take with me.

Squeezed in a tight and clumsy flight suit, I strained to catch a final glimpse of Bird Island. As we flew low over Teal Pond, Cobbler's Mound, Natural Arch, and other places dear to me, all of them seemed so small from the air and so remote at that moment.

Many thoughts raced through my brain as we sped toward the *Endurance*. Foremost among them was the one that I may have been mistaken in not accepting the invitation to stay on with my Bird Island companions, at least until the arrival of the next supply ship due several weeks from then. To have accepted the Fids' invitation, however, would have been selfish. Lönnberg House is equipped to handle four persons, not five, although Bruce had volunteered to sleep on the floor. Painful as it was, I knew that I had made the right decision, and I am sure that even now my companions agree. Field biologists understand only too well the consequences of over-accomodating.

Back in my old quarters on the *Endurance*, I basked in the luxury of hot showers, white table cloths, and fresh lettuce. All things shipside seemed familiar, except for the officers and men. They were new acquaintances, including the ship's master, Captain Derek Wallis of the Royal Navy.

My comfortable voyage on the *Endurance* soon ended. On 23 December, we sailed into King Edward Cove, the site of the South Georgian British Antarctic Survey base, where I transferred my belongings to *John Biscoe* in preparation for the return trip to the Falklands following the holidays. Christmas festivities were held on both ships as well as at the shore base. We made the rounds from one to the other, celebrating with our friends and thinking of our families who also would be observing Christmas and thinking of us. Mass was held in the chapel in the old whaling settlement of Grytviken. The Fids had kept the little church in good repair.

I spent my few remaining hours poking about in the screes of nearby mountains in search of storm petrels, which I failed to find. Beyond the huge reservoir that once serviced the whaling station, I explored upland areas I had somehow overlooked during previous trips to King Edward Cove. This new discovery proved to be a series of low, undulating hills, really dry fell-fields dominated by golden sedge grasses. On the hilltops and hillsides a few Antarctic terns nested. The single egg of one pair I found looked fresh, despite the late date.

LAST IMPRESSIONS

Between the yellow hills, saturated carpets of bright green moss overlay deep beds of peat. Undercutting the peat in many places, several swift-flowing glacial rivulets suddenly would drop from sight only to reappear at openings further downhill. Leaving behind the velvety bryophyte marshes, I climbed a steep seepage slope until I reached the rocky screes on the side of a mountain. In a rather level area where the scree was stable, I found eight tern nests, each with a single egg, within a few meters of one another. All eight were defended zealously. One of the more daring members of the little colony got so carried away with its dive-bombing tactics that I reached up and plucked it from the air.

Scattered along the base of the mountain was a much larger number of terns than I had realized existed at King Edward Cove. By the time I walked the lower edge of the screes to the end of the mountain overlooking a familiar alluvial plain called Hestesletten, I must have passed beneath several hundred angry terns, some isolated, others social in their nestings. Here, indeed, was an attractive study area for an equally attractive species.

Hestesletten is a birdy place, where two years before I had found my first burrows of prions and diving petrels by heeding the advice of Nigel Bonner. A fairly large glacial stream, the Penguin River, nearly bisects the plain in its swift but short-lived meanderings to the coast. Many elephant seals must have yawned and wallowed on its banks earlier in the season, but this day there were only a few.

Near the mouth of the Penguin River, several king penguins lined up so primly on a tiny gravel bar that I couldn't resist descending the mountain to photograph them. As I approached the kings, a pair of brown skuas flew in, the first I had seen all day, reminding me how scarce these predators were at King Edward Cove compared with Bird Island. Scarcer still were pipits; I saw not one.

Photographing the king penguins culminated my season's work, although I made some at-sea observations following *John Biscoe's* departure from King Edward Cove on 26 December. And when we passed the west end of South Georgia en route to the Falklands, I savored my last fleeting look at Bird Island.

Sailing the southern seas that last time aboard *John Biscoe* allowed me to reflect on the good life I had shared with the Fids. What had been a poor beginning in the pack ice off Palmer Station had certainly ended well. Now, after two years, it was finished. Not that I wouldn't see my British colleagues again—that would be highly improbable in a biologist's world of meetings and conclaves. But never again would I know the Fid's world as I had, never again have the same kinship.

134

Antarctic Tern

SELECTED BIBLIOGRAPHY

Bonner, W. Nigel. 1968. The Fur Seal of South Georgia. British Antarctic Survey
  Scientific Reports No. 56.

Conroy, J. W. H. 1972. Ecological aspects of the biology of the giant petrel, *Macronectes giganteus* (Gmelin), in the maritime Antarctic. *British Antarctic Survey
  Science Report*, 75, pp. 1-74.

Matthews, L. H. 1929. The birds of South Georgia. *Discovery Report*, 1, pp. 561-592.

Morris, R. O. 1962. Bird life in N. W. South Gerogia. *Sea Swallow*, 15, pp. 43-49.

Murphy, R. C. 1936. *Oceanic Birds of South America*. Volumes 1, 2, 1245 pp.,
  American Museum of Natural History, New York.

Prince, P. A. and M. R. Payne. 1979. Current status of birds at South Georgia. British
  Antarctic Survey Bulletin 48, pp. 103-118.

Rankin, N. 1951. *Antarctic Isle, Wildlife in South Georgia*, 383 pp., Collins, London.

Tickell, W. L. N. 1968. The biology of the great albatrosses, *Diomedea exulans* and
  Diomedea epomophora, in *Antarctic Bird Studies, Antarctic Research Series*,
  volume 12, edited by O. L. Austin, Jr., pp. 1-55, American Geophysical Union,
  Washington, D. C.

Watson, G. E. 1975. *Birds of the Antarctic and Sub-Antarctic*, 350 pp., American
  Geophysical Union, Washington, D. C.

Weller, M. W. 1975. Ecology and behavior of the South Georgian pintail (*Anas g.
  georgica*). *Ibis*, 117, pp. 217-231.

INDEX

References to illustrations and map place-names are set in **boldface type**.

INDEX

INDEX

Southern Ocean, **8**; boundaries of, 10
Specimens of birds, 103
Speckled teal, 73
Square Pond, **27**, 29, 131, 132
Square Pond peninsula, **15**
Squid, as food for albatross, 28
Stanley, Falkland Islands, 5, **8**, 17
Stanley greyhounds, 21, 133
Stercorariidae, 117
Stercorarius, 117
Sterna paradisaea, 128
Sterna vittata, 4. *See also* Antarctic tern
"Stinker," 83, 85. *See also* Giant petrel
Storm petrel: captured, 21; different species of, 22-23; feeding habits of, 86; on Shag Rocks, 99; vocalizations of, 110
Sutton, Professor George Miksch, 3: field biology, rules of, 31, 129
Swedish Antarctic Expedition, 14, 99
Swimming ability: of giant petrel, 86; of shag, 93; of skua, 126

Teal, speckled, 73
Teal Pond, **27**, **68**, 80: site of many birds, 78; beauty of, 81; mentioned, 105, 115, **120**, 133
Temperature changes at Antarctic Convergence, 9-10
Tern, 125, 134. *See also* Antarctic tern
Terra Australis Incognita, 7
Tickell, W. L. N., 52
Ticks on ocean birds, 57
Tierra del Fuego, **8**, 99, 126
Todd, E. P., 93
Tonk, **27**, 37, 50-51, 119: as nesting site for albatross, 28; skuas on, 121
Top Meadow, **27**, 29
Totipalmate condition, 93
Trios, of nesting birds, 107
Tristan da Cunha, skuas on, 118
Tussock grass: description of, 11, 27-28;

walking in, 26, 27-28; growth patterns of, 27; destruction of, by seals, 28, 45, 131; wetness of, 40; as material for nests, 75-76, 87, 90, 95, 112, 115, 131, **132**
Tussock hopping, 27-28
"Tussock isles," 5, 11

Ukkers, game of, 66-67
Ulva, 71
United States banding program, 128
United States Antarctic Research Program, 4, 14
United States Coast Guard, 103
University of Minnesota, radio telemetry techniques developed at, 129; mentioned, 4, 71, 118
USARP, 4, 14

Vegetation: of Bird Island, 9; of South Georgia, 10-11, 134; destroyed by seals, 28, 45, 131. *See also* Tussock grass
Vespucci, Amerigo, 7
Vocalizations: of white-chinned petrel, 18; of wildlife, 20; of pipit, 30; of northern giant petrel, 84; of blue-eyed shag, 96; of storm petrel, 110; of skua, 117

Wallis, Derek, Captain, 133
Wanderer. *See* Wandering albatross
Wanderer Ridge, **27**, 49, 56: home of wandering albatross, 45; as site of pools and birds, 78; as site of pipit nest, 115; as future site of skua study, 125
Wanderer Valley, 56
Wandering albatross, **24**, **44**, **46**, **47**, **49**, **55**, **56**, 86, 110, **120**: appearance of, 28, 52, **52**; feeding habits of, 28, **29**; nesting of, 45, 48, 50, 52-53; dominance of Bird Island by, 45-46; breeding of, 45-46, 51, 52, 54, 56; migration

range of, 46; wing span of, 46; flight of, 46, 47, **53**, 53-54, 55-56; banding of, 47; behavior in human presence, 47; mating of, 48-49; feet of, 49-50; egg of, 50; association with nesting giant petrel, 90-91, **91**. *See also* Albatross
Washington, state, skua migration to, 129
Watson, George, 42-43, 84, 112
Weather, effects on productivity and incubation of eggs, 89, 123. *See also* Climate
Weddell Sea, 8, **8**, 46
Welcome Islands, 7
Weller, Milton W., 71, 72
Whale: in food chain of Southern Ocean, 10; hunting of, 12, 13-14; as food for birds, 86
Whale research on South Georgia, 13
White-chinned petrel, **18**, **79**, 96: called "shoemakers," 18; burrows and egg of, 79; bite of, 79; behavior in human presence, 109. *See also* Petrel
White-rumped sandpiper, 131
Willis Islands, **11**, 18, **31**, **53**
Wilson's storm petrel, **23**, 110: breeding and eggs of, 23; migration of, 23; ejector of stomach oil, 85
Wind: in Southern Ocean, 10; around Bird Island, 32-33; and flight of sheathbills, 32; and flight of albatross, 34, 46; and giant petrel, 91
Wings: of gadfly petrels, 40; of wandering albatross and royal albatross, 46; of shag, 93; of skua, 117

Yellow-billed pintail, 69. *See also* Pintail, South Georgia

Zink, Robert, 43
"Zodiacs," rubber boats, 14, 100, 101
Zonibyx modestus, 17

140